This Is Not 'The End'

THIS IS NOT THE END.

STRATEGIES TO GET YOU THROUGH THE WORST CHAPTERS OF YOUR LIFE

NINA SOSSAMON-POGUE

NEW YORK

LONDON • NASHVILLE • MELBOURNE • VANCOUVER

This Is Not 'The End'

Strategies to Get You Through the Worst Chapters of Your Life

© 2020 Nina Sossamon-Pogue

Published in New York, New York, by Morgan James Publishing in partnership with Difference Press. Morgan James is a trademark of Morgan James, LLC.
www.MorganJamesPublishing.com

ISBN 9781642798067 paperback
ISBN 9781642798074 eBook
Library of Congress Control Number: 2019950065

Cover Design Concept:
Jennifer Stimson

Cover & Interior Design by:
Christopher Kirk
www.GFSstudio.com

Editor:
Todd Hunter

Book Coaching:
The Author Incubator

Internal Graphics by:
Sara Alarcon

Morgan James is a proud partner of Habitat for Humanity Peninsula and Greater Williamsburg. Partners in building since 2006.

Get involved today! Visit
MorganJamesPublishing.com/giving-back

Table of Contents

CHAPTER 1:

THIS Was Not Part of Your Plan

"Sometimes life hits you like a brick in the face"
– Steve Jobs

Well this is a crappy way to meet you. If you've picked up this book, you are probably dealing with some unwanted or unexpected event in your life. Something that was not at all what you planned. You wake up in the morning and for a brief moment wonder if it is possible that you have had a really bad dream, and then the memories flood your mind. Those memories start their daily invasion of your head and the reality sets in again. Throughout the day you may feel sad, angry, or lost at any moment. You just can't understand how this could have happened and you aren't sure what you are supposed to do next. Maybe this 'thing' was something that was within your control or maybe it happened to you; either way, it is taking up your waking thoughts and is becoming part of your life story. And, you do *not* want it to be part of your story. If someone was writing a book about your life, you don't want these pages to be part of it. I hear ya! That's why I wrote this book.

Since whatever you are dealing with is unique to you, I am going to call your horrible thing that you are trying to deal with *THIS*. You may not say it out loud, but THIS Sucks! THIS isn't fair, THIS isn't you, you had a plan, and THIS is not the way your life was supposed to go. I am going to assume that you are a good person or sometimes try to be a good person; that you are not an ax murderer; and that and you do some nice things. With that, we can rant further, I mean there are a lot of people who do lots of crappy things, and THIS didn't happen to them. Really?! What about those really horrible jerks who rob and steal and hurt people or take advantage of others or kick adorable puppies. Those people might deserve THIS, but not you. How come your life feels ruined?

I am strangely fascinated with how many situations cause THIS. When I was a television reporter, I saw THIS on public display following traumatic accidents and in politics, courtrooms, and sports almost daily. Traumatic loses change lives. Each THIS is unique, but when you take a step back they often play out in one of these ways:

- You worked really hard for a long time to get to a milestone in your life and it just didn't work out. You're thinking, how can it just be over and you didn't get to where you wanted to be?
- You were going about your life and then THIS happened. Maybe THIS is an accident or an illness or something completely out of your control.
- You committed to and planned something for a long time. You've been overjoyed and excited, envisioning what was going to happen and it was going to be so fantastic after all this time, but THIS, this horrible thing, happened instead.

People are always reminding us that we "only have one life." So, did you just waste a big chunk of it? Did THIS just derail your whole life?

I think most of us feel like THIS is some horrible thing that happens to other people. You did all the right things (well most of them). It makes no sense that THIS is now part of your life story. You are thinking, "How did I end up here? How could things go so wrong? How in the world will my life ever be the same?

THIS Is Changing Everything

You may have realized that THIS is not just affecting you. The people around you are acting differently, and you may be worried they are going to remember you for THIS – for forever. Is THIS who you are now? Will THIS be how you are remembered? You know you are so much more and you certainly don't want THIS to be the first thing people think about when they think of you. It may feel too late. People are already looking at you differently. Some may be feeling sorry for you and some are doing all they can to help you. You just want your friendships and relationships to go back to the way they were when THIS wasn't part of the conversation.

Here's some good news. Your thoughts about THIS are normal. You are not alone. When we have a plan for our lives and are headed in a direction that we feel is right, and then we are abruptly jolted in another direction, it does seem as if the entirety of our lives has come off the track. When THIS happens, everything in our world seems to change. I am guessing that whatever your THIS is, it is taking up a large part of your every waking moment. Not one day or even one hour gets to be like it was before THIS. Sometimes you start to feel normal, but then someone or something reminds you that THIS really did happen and the memories flood your mind. You relive THIS over and over. A simple "How are you doing" becomes impossible to answer.

I'll say it: THIS SUCKS! You probably just want to escape this really horrible chapter of your life. You want to go back and somehow get a do-over. If you had a time machine that could take you back to a time before THIS, then you could do things differently. If only you knew The Flash! Yes, and you would understand the speed force, so you could go back in time and get a do-over and fix everything. (If you are not a superhero fan, he's the really fast guy who can outrun the time continuum and go back in time. He tries to fix things with do-overs.)

You may also feel like time itself feels different now. How long has THIS been engulfing you? How long has it been filling your usually joyful soul with sludge? THIS can cause you to question if life will ever be OK. It's interrupting even the few moments of calm that you desperately need in your day. THIS will do that.

There's No Space for THIS in Your Head

Before THIS, you probably didn't realize the amount of space that a horrible event can take up in someone's brain. The memory is constantly swirling in your head, trying to fit in. It might even seem like it's growing each day. The problem is, THIS doesn't fit in with the story of your life that you have been creating. It's like it's a horror story in a romance novel or maybe it's written in a foreign language and the rest of the book is in English. THIS just doesn't fit in your book. Sometimes I picture that our brains are full of doors of all shapes and sizes and THIS is some oddity that is too big and weirdly shaped to fit into any of those doors, so it keeps opening every door trying to find a home but getting shut out. You may have your own visual image of how THIS doesn't fit. For some, THIS is an ugly, hideous thing and they are frightened that it now has to be a part of them.

THIS Is Important

I hate that you are struggling with whatever your THIS is, but I am glad you picked up this book during this crappy chapter of your life. As much as you don't want THIS to be a part of you or part of your life story, it is becoming a big part. You are going to have to find a place for THIS to settle in. You don't have to welcome it with open arms and make it part of your "happy place" (ugh, I will talk about that concept later), but you do have to translate it and make it fit in somehow. Let's think of it this way: if your life is this big thick book about you, these are a few pages in that big book that you can't rip out. As it turns out, they are very important pages. They are the unexpected plot twist that leads to character development, introduces new characters, and takes your story in a new direction. I want to show you that your story can still be a really good story and there are many more chapters that follow this crappy chapter.

If you rip out the few pages that make up this crappy chapter because you don't like them, your whole book will never make sense. As horrible as THIS is, this is the chapter that explains how you turn out in the end. This is the chapter that actually makes you stronger, smarter, and happier. I know right – I am so full of crap! There is no way that THIS horrible thing that is happening to you right now could be anything but terrible for your future. I hear you, but stick with me. I get that your THIS is different and that there are people who say, "I know what you're going through" or "I know how you feel" and those people irritate the crap out of you. In the middle of my THIS, I told a perfectly kind person "No you don't 'expletive' know how I feel – THIS is not happening to you" (not my finest moment).

CHAPTER 2:

Life Is a Series of Plot Twists

"We don't receive wisdom; we must discover it for ourselves after a journey that no one can take for us or spare us."
– Marcel Proust

Five Failures

One: I wish I had known how long my life story would be when I was sixteen and lying in the back of my coach's Porsche. Those are the first pages I wanted to rip out of the story of my life.

I was still in my red USA sweats, curled up in a fetal position, and we were headed home from that national qualifying meet. I was trying to cry quietly so my coach couldn't hear me. He was upset too because this was his chance to coach another Olympian. He had been there before. He had put a lot of time, literally years, and energy into my training. He could have chosen any talented girl he wanted, and he had chosen me. And I blew it. As we drove back toward home, I tried to get my head around THIS. Just a few weeks before THIS, I had been on the cover of a magazine with the words "Maryland's Olympic Hopeful" next to my face. I'd been training since I was five and now my dream of making the 1984 Olympic team would never come true. THIS could not be happening. I thought my life was over.

I dreaded having to face my parents who had given up so much for me. They had invested so much time and money and had moved from Florida to Maryland for my training. I thought about my brothers and sister, who had their lives changed by my training. How could I face my family after such a failure? And school! I was going to have to walk down the halls at my high school and see all those faces. For years, the other students at my high school were subjected to morning announcements about "Nina competing in Japan this weekend" and "Check out Nina on ABC Sports this Saturday "or "Congratulations to Nina who won a big gymnastics meet over the weekend". Ugh, school was going to be a nightmare. In my sixteen-year-old head lying in the back of the car, each mile we drove toward home was taking me closer to what I dreaded most. Everyone would know THIS. I had failed. While some would feel sorry for me (which was bad enough), others would be secretly glad that I fell off the bars and bombed the meet. I was sure they would think, *After all that hype, she wasn't good enough.*

Two: I made it through that last year of high school. I'll share more on that later. I knew college could be a fresh start, and I was still a top college recruit. I chose Louisiana State University, which had a top gymnastics program and was far away from anyone I knew. I made a plan to work hard and make LSU proud. I liked the thought of a fresh start and new friends. In college, I found myself surrounded by other top athletes who had given up much of their young lives to become great at their sport. They understood me. My new friends also had stories of brutal training schedules, tough coaches, and regrets about spending so much of their teenage lives in a gym. We got each other. I felt like my life was going to be OK. Then, during a competition near the end of my freshman year, I was in the middle of my beam routine in a competition. I was feeling confident. It was a really solid routine. I felt strong and decided to throw a more difficult dismount than we had planned. My coach had specifically told me to hold off on the harder dismount 'til later in the season, but I felt great! I had this!

Throwing her guidance out the window, I gave it all I had. I was plenty high enough to complete the flip and the twist, and I was coming down toward the mat and … and I didn't bend my knees enough when I landed. My left knee looked like an old stick shift in a standard car. The bottom part of my leg planted in the ground with the top part grinding in a circle around it. I blew out my knee in all directions. It was a bad. Those who witnessed it later told me I yelled several profanities, really loud. I deny that I ever shouted that in a public arena full of little girls. The next day on the front page of the *Daily Reveille*, the LSU college paper, the headline read, "another one bites the dust." The accompanying photo showed me on my back grabbing my knee with both hands, grimacing while the coaches and paramedics held me down. Major knee surgery followed, and the doctor told me if I wanted to have a healthy leg as an adult, it was best that I didn't do gymnastics anymore. THIS was not happening. I quickly went from a top NCAA recruit to working in the athletic department laundry room, on crutches, to keep my scholarship. I am pretty sure I washed Shaquille O'Neil's jock strap. THIS was not part of my plan, and I certainly didn't want washing Shaq's jock strap to be my claim to fame.

I had to find something to replace gymnastics and lucky for me there was an abundant supply of cute boys and cold beer at LSU. I went through my college years, falling in love, drinking beer, and making OK grades. Looking back,

I could have handled it much better. I think I just kept busy and tried not to think too hard about too much. I just took each day as it came. Maybe that's a survival skill in itself, but not the healthiest way to survive. There were a few people who helped me. I will talk about them later.

Fortunately for me, one of those cute boys I dated was a personal trainer whose client was the wife of the owner of the local TV station. With that good luck going for me, I got an internship at WBRZ-TV.

A New Passion

I loved the newsroom. After just a few days, I knew I had found my new passion. Working in news each day was a new rush of information. In the news business you covered stories of individuals experiencing amazing highs and devastating lows. I spent the next fifteen years in television, covering countless shootings, stabbings, and horrible car accidents. I also saw athletes break records, politicians win elections and met lottery winners. I would be sent to cover the national hot air balloon championships and ride in balloons. I once rode an elephant down the interstate when the circus came to town, and I rode in a hurricane-tracking plane over the Gulf of Mexico into the eye of Hurricane Andrew after it hit Florida and before it reached Louisiana. I loved the intensity of the news business. For all the years I did news, I worked hard to improve each day and tried to always be genuine. I tried to tell stories with compassion and honesty. I doubled checked facts to be sure my reporting was fair, balanced, and accurate, just like they taught in journalism school. Each night I tried to connect with the viewers and tell a well thought out story.

My news career took me to Charleston, South Carolina, where I became the evening news anchor and fell in love with the Lowcounty, and in turn the Lowcountry fell in love with me. I anchored three shows a day. I jumped in to help charities, spoke at schools, and took part in all the ribbon cuttings in town. The Charleston viewers watched as I got big during my pregnancies and then celebrated the births of my children with me. They voted me Charleston's favorite news anchor for seven years running. I had found my place. I was back on top!

Three: One Friday afternoon as I was walking to the studio to record a news brief the general manager asked to see me. It was the day after the "Charleston's Best" awards were in the paper, so I assumed the GM was going to say thanks and maybe give me a bonus! That didn't happen. We sat down in his office and he called in a young woman from HR. Then he looked at me across the desk and said, "We are releasing you from your contract, without cause, effective immediately." That sentence is all I remember him saying. I asked, "Have I done something wrong?" He said "No, we are releasing you from your contract, without cause, effective immediately." I was crushed. (Later in life, I realized the legal process that goes along with budget cuts and forced attrition, but at the time I was hurt and confused),"

Obviously firing a popular TV anchor could cost the TV station some ratings points, so they had a plan for that. I was told they would shorten my noncompete clause from one year to six months. The six months would be paid in full, as long as I agreed to not talk about the terms of the separation for one year. If asked, I would say that this was a mutual decision. Sitting in his office it became clear that my departure was nonnegotiable, the young HR woman had already gotten my purse from my desk, and she walked me to my car. I was devastated. THIS could not be happening. Alone in my car in the TV station parking lot, I had no idea what to do or where to go. I couldn't go home; the babysitter was there, and I couldn't handle kids right now. I couldn't go anywhere in town – I felt like everyone would wonder why I was dressed for the news and not on the air. I drove toward the beach, stopped at my parents' (I was thankful they weren't home), took a pair of sneakers from the bottom of my mom's closet (a half size too small for me), and drove to Sullivan's Island. I walked for hours that afternoon. I was sure my life as I knew it was over.

My Life Is Like a Country Song

Four: From the outside, you might think, *Still, she had healthy kids and a loving family*. Well that did look good from the outside, but behind closed doors, we were struggling. That part of my plan for my life was not going as planned either. My marriage fell apart that year too, and I was sure I had ruined my three- and five-year-olds lives as well as my own. Divorce/THIS was the end of my dreams of family vacations and Christmas mornings with all of us together. But, wait, there's more! I might as well tell it all. I had a black lab named Douglas who was the best dog you could ever imagine. He could catch a Frisbee while running full speed on the beach. Douglas had been with me since my senior year of college. That same year, the vet told me he had a large tumor and the humane thing to do would be to put him down. His last night, we cooked him a steak on the grill and I slept in his bed with him. The next day, I held him as they put him to sleep. It felt like my world was crumbling. I had planned a much better life story and had worked so hard. How had my life become THIS. I was a character in a sad country song – *I lost my job, my marriage fell apart, and my dog died... doo-ah, doo-dah.*

New TV Station

I spent the next six months thinking about how my life went so wrong and trying to figure out a path forward. I realized I loved the Lowcountry and I still loved news. When my noncompete clause expired, I went to the TV station down the street and got a job. The main anchor there was already a friend of mine. He thought it was a great idea too. We decided we would make a great team. Lucky for me, the station was looking for a new female lead, and I was willing to make less money to just be back on my feet.

Over the years, my coanchor and I became good friends. We were comfortable on the air together, and the ratings went up. The viewers liked us together and they voted me Charleston's Favorite News Anchor for the tenth time. I also won an Emmy for best news anchor in the Southeast. I was back on top of my game – then came the most devastating plot twist of my life.

Five: This is tough to even write about. I honestly don't want to put the images of this THIS in your head any more than I want those memories in my mind. There was a woman who witnessed it from a window across the street, and she wet her pants and almost passed out before she could call 911. THIS chapter almost ended my story.

Almost 'The End'

October 3, 2005

It was a sunny afternoon. You could hear the kids on the school bus as it came down the street. Usually, I would be in the newsroom at this time, but I had taken the day off so I could meet the bus and be a 'regular mom' for the day. The school bus stop was in front of my coanchor's home, which was down the street and around the corner from ours. I had driven over a little early so I could spend some time catching up with his wife, who was a good friend. We sat on the lawn in the sun and chatted while their youngest son, Sam, crawled around in the grass next to us. At eleven months, Sam was getting good at crawling. All three of my friend's boys were cute, but Sam was adorable – sweet, round face and all smiles. When the bus stopped, about a dozen elementary school kids poured out with their backpacks, still chatting with each other. It was great to see my son Jake's smiling face. I envied all the moms who got to see this play out each day. Jake and her son Jack were eight, and they liked to run around after school. But this day, we both had things to do and didn't have time for them to play together. So we said our goodbyes and I called Jake to get in the car. My friend started to gather up her boys to head inside. From my car window, I remember thinking fall was in the air, everyone was happy, and I was so thankful to be right there, right then. That is the last happy thought I can recall. Nothing is the same after that. Somehow Sam had crawled onto the driveway and as I went to leave his sweet beautiful head ended up under my front tire. Adults and children screamed. She and I ran to him. It all moved fast. There was no time to wait for an ambulance. I remember driving as fast as that car could go, blaring the horn, both of us in some out-of-body experience, beyond any emotion I can put into words. We drove right up to the sliding doors of the hospital. I remember jumping out yelling, "Come NOW - get him. NOW!" And I remember the rush of doctors heading towards us. They took him and I slumped down against the wall.

I couldn't tell you exactly what I was thinking then. The commotion was all too much. But I'm pretty sure somewhere in the horror, panic, grief, guilt, and despair, I knew THIS was it. Life would never be OK again for any of us.

In the weeks that followed, I wondered how had I gone from Olympic hopeful and Charleston's favorite news anchor to the lady who ran over her friend's baby. There was no way to fix it. I could see no way forward after THIS.

CHAPTER 3:

The Story of Your Life

"Show me someone who has done something
worthwhile, and I'll show you someone
who has overcome adversity."
– Lou Holtz

Eight years after the accident with Sam, just two weeks to the date, I found myself in New York City on the Nasdaq showroom floor preparing for the opening bell. Now a vice president in a high-growth software company, I was part of a team that was pulling off one of the most successful Tech IPO's of 2013. How in the world did I get there? How did I get out of that harrowing chapter of my life that followed the accident with Sam? Where did I find the strength to go on? Did that strength play a part in this new success? I didn't know the answers to those questions at the time. But I think I do now and I think they can help you.

THIS has unseen consequences, both bad and good. What I have learned through my own crappy chapters that played out in very public ways is an odd collection of life experiences combined with the hundreds of books and articles I have read to try to make sense of it. It is a strange mix of learnings that I have tried to organize into bite size chapters for you. With today's social media, you don't have to be an Olympic hopeful or a TV personality to experience public pain. Everyone's major life events are played out in public. You have the trauma of an event then the trauma of the public scrutiny. I feel like the coping skills I developed during my very public life are needed now more than ever.

Your THIS

I can only imagine what your THIS is that you are struggling with. Your THIS may make my crappy chapters seem a lot less crappy. There are so many folks who experience major life events that consume them. Whatever your THIS is, I just want to share some things that I think can help you successfully come out on the other side of it. I am proof that it is possible that THIS will not define you and that you can go on to have great success. Most of the people I work with every day don't know about the accident with Sam or about any of my crappy chapters. They just think I am successful, and they probably think that I'm happy all the time.

I am not a psychology expert on failure and trauma or an academic who studies stoic philosophy. What I am is a person who has experienced a lot of highs and lows in my life talking to you as if you are a good friend, or a friend of a friend, or a work colleague. If you were one my kids' college friends going through a really tough time, I would find a comfy spot on a couch, a corner table in a café or sit on the end of a dock and tell these same stories and share these same tips. Now I am sure some very enlightened person is going to read this and will want to explain to me the deeper meaning or the science of the brain in these situations. Please do. Get in touch with me and let's talk. I love to learn. However, this book is for all of you who just need to survive THIS. I am not going to dig into the science of it; I am just going to share some things that work.

To do this, I am going to stick with the book analogy – this idea that you are the author of your own life story and you cannot rip out these pages. With that, think of THIS thing that you are going through as a horrible plot twist in the story of your life. Since it is not what you planned, you are going to have to write yourself out of it. Imagine your book for a moment. How big is it? What color is the cover?

If you flipped it open to the page that is today where do you find that? Is that towards the beginning of the book? Is it in the middle? I'm here to tell you it's not THE END.

In the 7 chapters ahead, I share some practical strategies and things to do to get through this crappy chapter. I used to think that other people just knew these things and then realized most don't. Why would they? We aren't taught this and even the people writing the psych journals are still figuring out how our brains work. As I've helped others who were struggling, I've realized that you have to actually go through THIS to get it and everyone's struggle is unique. It became clear to me that we don't develop these coping skills unless we need them. The more we need them, the stronger those coping muscles become. Some lucky people may never develop them, which would be great I guess, until of course they have a horrible plot twist and they need them. That's why I've put them into a book for easy access.

I am not downplaying any events, but I've simplified them. I felt it was important to tell stories and make these ideas simple, because when you are in the middle of a crushing chapter in your life, you need plain language, and someone to tell you a few practical things to do to get through the day. When you are going through THIS, you don't have the energy or capacity to consume a large psychology journal or workbook. I know there are a ton of wonderful books out there that deal with failure, anxiety, trauma, PTSD, suicide, and the many therapies to deal with them. I once stood in the aisle at Barnes & Noble and stared at the self-help section searching for anything to help. As I did so, I just got sadder and felt defeated. There were big science journals and workbooks, and there were books about someone else's problems. They were all too much. I had my own truckload of crap to deal with, and it was too heavy a load to move forward. This is the book I wanted. I started to call it "Don't let this thing consume you – grab this book." I thought about writing that in big red letters so you would find it.

Seven Coping Skills/Tools

In the next seven chapters, I will explain some coping skills and share tools that will help you get from where you are now to a better chapter. I'll share some things that helped me; plus, I have read a ton of books searching for answers, so I will give you the CliffNotes (SparkNotes depending on your generation) version of things you probably would read if you felt up to it.

First, I will help you figure out how you fit THIS into your head. I know you don't want to, so I will ease you into that. You will be urged to take a hard look at how you are thinking about THIS and how you are talking about it. You'll learn how to choose the words you are using to describe THIS and how you can make THIS part of your life story in a way that works for you.

You will learn to examine all the people and places around you right now. It is important to look at who is really helping you and who might be hurting you. You might need to create some space to give yourself a break. If you just got fired or divorced, you'll need to think about who you are venting to. If you have suffered a tragedy, I will give you some ideas about how to sort through the people and places that might trigger a downward spiral that you didn't see coming.

One of my favorite parts of this book is an interesting concept about time that can help you look at your life in new ways. An old boyfriend shared this concept with me twenty-two years after we broke up. We went to dinner twenty-two years later and had this deep, weird conversation about emotions and time. I wish I had this little pearl of knowledge sooner in my life. It can help you put THIS in perspective, and you may look at your life in a new way when you consider this crappy chapter as a percentage of the whole of your life story. If you don't read this whole book, just check out Chapter 6. I love this concept.

To have success in the future, you will have to let go of some ideas or some magical thinking you may have about the future. I'll help you learn how to look at the old, pre-THIS you and the new post-THIS you. We can create some new magic and miracles, by using a few mental hacks to help you envision a future where THIS isn't crushing you.

The really horrible stuff going on in your head can be frightening. Getting past the "my life is ruined" from a trauma and the "my life is ruined" from divorce are very different, but the coping skills are similar. I am going to assume that some of you reading this may have thought about harming yourself or checking out. Your mind can go there when THIS is consuming you and you see no way forward. I've been there. I have come inches from stepping into traffic. I really hope you will read Chapter 8.

The most valuable tool in my coping toolbox is in Chapter 9. One of the hardest things to do is to get back out into the world after THIS. If you feel like you can't leave the safety of your own home because a simple "How's it going?" is an impossible question to answer, I have a tool for that. What do you say? What are people thinking? I have some practical next steps. I'll show you how to create a script that empowers you to step out into the world and gives you back some control.

Since I am sure there are parts of you and your life that you wish didn't have to change and the months ahead seem so uncertain, I have included some ideas on how you affect the future. We will look at the things that make you smile and things that make you crazy and create a plan to add or drop those in the next chapter of your life. It may seem unrealistic right now, but I'll help you start toward a future that is uniquely what you desire.

Here is the deal, unless you are Marty McFly and you and Doc have figured out the flux capacitor and built a time machine out of a DeLorean ('80s movie reference), then you can't go back and do things differently. You are going to have to figure a way out of this crappy chapter of your life. To do that, you are going to have to start thinking past THIS. In other words, there was a you before THIS interrupted the life you were leading and there will be a you after. By the end of this book, you will start to believe in the you after THIS. And I don't want to spoil the big finish – but it's a pretty cool concept of you.

CHAPTER 4:

You Are the Main Character

"There's no 'should' or 'should not' when it comes to having feelings. They're part of who we are and their origins are beyond our control. When we can believe that, we may find it easier to make constructive choices about what to do with those feelings."
– Mr. Rogers

T HIS is super difficult and it sucks. For some, the first thing to tackle to get through this crappy chapter can be the hardest. You need to start with THIS oddity that is too big and weirdly shaped and is swirling around in your mind trying to find a place to fit in. You are going to have to find a place for it somehow. You are going to have to figure out how THIS goes into the book that is your story. I am pretty sure you don't want to. You feel it's not fair that you have to, but we are going to figure out how this crappy chapter fits in.

I Don't Want THIS – College Laundry Room

When I was nineteen, I would sit on the ground outside the athletic department laundry room at LSU and watch the other athletes headed to practice pass by. In my head, I still wanted to be one of them. I could not accept that this injury now meant that I was no longer an athlete. All I wanted to be was one of those D1 athletes representing my school and competing in the sport that I had spent my life trying to perfect. My reality was that I was on crutches, in charge of washing jock straps, and I was never going to be that again. The never part was too much for me to digest. Gymnastics had been the focus of my life since I was five. My identity was tied to it. It was on all my sweatshirts and T-shirts and on the bumper sticker of my car. If it were today, it would be my Twitter account and Instagram page. It was the first thing that I would say when describing myself: "I'm a gymnast." To go from top NCAA recruit and LSU gymnast to the girl working in the laundry room was a reality that did NOT fit in my head. It was not acceptable.

The laundry room was in the Pete Maravich Assembly Center (PMAC), a big auditorium where the basketball team played and touring bands held concerts. The door to the laundry room was on the outside of the auditorium. Athletes, coaches, trainers, and hundreds of people associated with LSU athletics walked by there each day. Some said hello, but most rushed passed without noticing me or avoided eye contact. I suppose it was a sad scene, and I was likely not giving off a good vibe. I would have avoided me too.

One afternoon an athletic advisor happened to stop and chat. Of course, I told him that I was fine. I was glad to have a scholarship and I probably made a joke about washing jock straps. No, I didn't need to go to his office or anything. When I look back now, I think he was the only one who may have known I was in trouble. He came by more than once, he would stop and sit on the warm pavement with me and lean up against the building. He would get me talking about what I might want to do after college. He got me thinking about working in the other roles in the athletic department. He told me about sports information and what courses it would take to switch to a journalism degree. He became a person I looked forward to seeing and someone I found myself cautiously starting to talk about the future with. Talking about it made it real and I desperately wanted it to be a bad dream and to wake up and still be a gymnast.

I was hanging on to that and I don't think I actually went to his office until a year after my injury, when I was walking and doing better. As I look back at my life story, he's the one who taught me this first lesson: you are different now and you have to start thinking of the next version of you.

The idea that there is a you before THIS and there is a you after THIS is so hard to see when you are in it. That is what causes so much pain. We don't want to give up the old version of ourselves, so we hold on for our lives. We don't like the thought of a new version, nor do we want to imagine a life with that version of us. But here we are with these few new pages in the book of our life and we can't rip them out, so the next chapter is going to have something in it, and the main character is going to be a little different than he or she was in the last chapter.

I Don't Want THIS – Divorce Changes Everything

When I got divorced, everything I had envisioned for my life felt ruined. Those chapters that I had already written in my mind had family vacations, family holidays, and happily-ever-after scenarios. They would not become my story and that life I had envisioned was ruined. The words *ruined* and *never* seem to come up a lot in the pages of your story when life changing plot twists are pulling you under. Divorce meant that I would never have a Christmas with everyone together again; I would never have my kids all the time. I would be one of "those divorced women" who no one wants their husbands to be around. Our heads do some crazy stuff to us when we go through THIS. However, when I was getting divorced in my mid-thirties, the concept of "ruined" did not deliver the fatal blow it might have to others. Some place deep inside, I think that nineteen-year-old version of me leaning up against the laundry room wall knew better. My life wasn't ruined. It was absolutely never going to be the same, but being divorced was not going to define me any more than no longer being gymnast did. I leaned into the thought that I had had a lot of great times and a good marriage for a while. I looked at my reality, which was that I had beautiful children and lived in a town I loved. I decided I would figure out what the divorced version of me was going to be like. At some point, I actually made a list. Things that I wanted to change, to do, to improve. In the years that followed, I became a better version of myself. I painted murals on the kids' new rooms. I parented like I had always wanted to. I ate healthier, worked out, and took care of myself. I was a better mom and liked myself better. It wasn't easy, and I was often sad. Your emotions are all over the place during a divorce. I lost some friends along the way. Divorce does that. But I was somehow sure that I would make new friends and those people would be more like the new me. They would like to do the things I liked to do and go to the same parks or playgrounds with the kids. I came to terms with the fact that I was never going to be married to my kids' dad again and that we were never going to be that forever family that I had in my head. I decided that was OK. That permission gave me license to be anything I wanted. That change is actually an important thing to note: When big life events happen, you have the opportunity to change. People won't question why or push back. It is almost expected.

You Are Causing Your Pain

I share those stories because what you are saying to yourself now probably needs to change. We fight to accept THIS as it swirls around in our heads looking for a place to settle. When you wake up tomorrow hoping this was a bad dream, THIS is still going to be your reality. You have to open a door for it. There is a great book called *Self Coaching 101*. In it, Brooke Castillo explains it this way: "No matter how horrific your past, no matter how horrible the event, the only thing that ever causes us emotional pain is our story (thoughts) about it." The author goes on to say, "So to be very clear: Right now, what is painful about your past is your current thought. Period."

That's the splash of cold water on your face. If you hurt right now, it's because you continue to beat yourself up with your thoughts. To stop that kind of self-injury, you need to come up with a different thought about THIS. Your thoughts are completely within your control.

Ugh – I know that it sucks to hear that you are doing this to yourself, and it seems so unfair that you have to figure out how to do this, but that's the deal. I've skinnied down her self-coaching model to make a quick fix for you:

Start with what you are saying to yourself right now.

What is your original thought? Here are some examples:

- I blew it and will never get hired again
- I am getting a divorce and my life will never be what I wanted
- I lost my wife, and it is all people see when they look at me
- I tanked my company and ruined everyone's lives
- I caused a horrible accident, and no one will ever forget it
- I lost my baby, and I can't ever be happy again
- I made an embarrassing, fool of myself, and I can't face the world

We say the worst things to ourselves in our heads. We beat ourselves up with things most people would never say out loud. Some of what we say is simply not true. Some of it is only our opinion. Most of the time, the stuff going on in your head is worse than what's really happening.

Here's your work for this chapter – One way to think about how you are talking to yourself is to take yourself out of it and figure out what you would say if THIS had happened to a child. What would you say to that child to comfort them?

Write it down.

Next, you probably have people around you who are saying nice things to you and comforting you, but you can't hear them. I get it. That self-talk in your head is too loud for anyone to get through. They might be saying things like:

- *It's going to be OK. I'm so sorry that you are going through this*
- *You of all people don't deserve this*
- *I am here for you*
- *I wish I could take the pain away*

You need to quiet the self-talk in your head that is drowning out everything else, so you can hear them. Write down what they are actually saying.

Now, think about how you are talking to yourself and add some additional filters to figure out a way to be kinder to yourself. Here is the skinnied down *Self Coaching 101* concept to create a quick fix version for you.

First – Write down your original thought about THIS? (don't skip the crazy – this is what are you really saying to yourself in your head)

Now add these filters and write responses:

- What's not factual/only your opinion?
- What would you say to a friend?
- What is a nicer thing to say to yourself?

With those answers, write yourself a new thought about THIS.

This quick writing task can help you make THIS part of your story in a way that you can accept it. If you actually take a moment to write a few things down now, you are literally beginning to rewrite your story. How you think about THIS and talk about it to yourself becomes how you talk to about THIS to others. The words you take time to choose will become the story of this chapter in your life. You are the author.

Good News/Bad News

Now, let me give you some good news bad news. I'll start with the bad news, which I've already told you, but I'll say it again: **You cannot go back to the old you**. Too much character development has happened. The main character in your life story is going through some serious character development, and there has to be a new version of you going forward. The good news is that you get to create this new version. I discuss this more in Chapter 10.

This first step is your call. I am going to assume that you do not want to stay where you are, be damaged goods, or be defined by THIS for forever. You may be sad, mad, frustrated, and scared. You can keep all that grief, shame, and fear because it is all real. You can both feel all the emotions you need to feel AND decide to be something stronger on the other side of THIS.

After the accident with Sam, I could not figure out how to fit world-class athlete and beloved news anchor in the same head with lady who ran over a baby. There was no way that was going to be OK. It took a good therapist and some time before I could find a place for it. I will share more on that in Chapter 8. For this task – here is what this exercise would have looked like for me in the days after the accident with Sam.

My original thought: My life is over, I have killed someone, I am going to be remembered as the lady who ran over the baby for the rest of my life. I have forever shattered my friends' lives. People would be better off without me.

- What's not factual – Sam was alive. He was undergoing surgeries and his chances of survival were increasing. My friends were struggling, but they were a strong couple and would hold tight to each other.
- What would you say to a friend – You are a good person, this was an accident, he is going to pull through and you are going to be OK.
- What is a nicer thing to say to yourself – I was part of a horrible accident. It doesn't make sense, but somehow we can all get through this and life goes on.

New thought: My life will never be the same. This was an accident, and it has changed us all, but we are going to be OK somehow.

Take a moment to do this exercise for yourself before going on to the next chapter. Focus on your main character – you, before bringing in the supporting cast of characters. Start choosing the words that you can say out loud and finding a place for THIS in your head. How are you going to refer to it going forward? You can start being kinder to yourself right now. This quick writing exercise will help you stop beating yourself up with your own thoughts and creates the dialogue that you and everyone around you will use going forward.

CHAPTER 5:

Choose Your Cast of Characters Wisely

"You are what you are by what you believe."
– Oprah

So enough about me, what do you think of me? I sometimes say that joke when I find myself sharing all my problems and stuff with my family or friends. It's sort of the crux of this next tip. You are consumed by THIS, and you are thinking that the people all around you are talking about THIS. You are pretty sure it is top of mind for everyone you meet. Well I assure you that THIS is not taking up as much space in other people's heads as it is in yours. It may be horrible or sad or unfair or whatever words you use to label THIS, so it seems like it should be on everyone's minds all the time, but it's not. THIS is only on full volume for you. Most people are tuned to their own internal radio station of WAME – What About ME radio.

You may find it hard to grasp right now, but even our closest friends and family don't take THIS on like we do. The cast of characters around you during this time is also dealing with their own emotions and issues, and they may be pulling some extra weight while you are not at full capacity. They are thinking about you, but they are not consumed with THIS like you are. The people around you become an important part of your story, only when you let them.

You will need some people to help you. At the same time, you may need to keep others at a distance. Even some of the people who love you the most and those who are "in it with you" might make things worse. This chapter will help you consider how other people are actually thinking about THIS and determine who is helping or hurting you.

Facing the Halls of My High School

When my sixteen-year-old self walked down the halls of my high school after blowing my shot at the Olympic team, she was miserable. I was sure everyone saw me as a failure. They were either feeling sorry for me or laughing at me. Both felt the same. At first, I tried to get from class to class without making eye contact. I would leave for lunch alone to get away from it. For the remainder of my time in high school, I always felt like it was the first thing people thought of when they saw me. When I graduated I didn't stay in close contact with many people from high school. I didn't make many close friends anyway because I was always training in the gym while they were out being teenagers. Twenty years after high school graduation, I was invited to go back to my high school and be inducted into the school's new athletic hall of fame. At first, I was surprised by this and was hesitant to go back. I had not stepped foot in my old high school since graduation. I flew back to my hometown and went to the event. When I saw the plaque on the wall with my name on it, I was once again that embarrassed teenager who had failed to make the Olympic team. But, wait. The people I interacted with over the next few hours didn't seem to remember it that way. They introduced me as "the best gymnast we've ever had" and said, "She almost made the Olympics! We were all so proud to know her."

What?!? How could they have it so wrong? I bombed! I was a huge loser!! At first, I could not wrap my head around this new description of my life. My life story that I had been telling myself, and which I was sure others were also telling, was very different from the story my old schoolmates were recounting.

I had written that very painful chapter all by myself. No one else had that story in his or her head. They had heard those announcements or saw me in the hall and their thoughts likely went something like this: "Gymnast, Nina, bla, bla, bla, bla, bla, bla, math test, there is cute boy, their own drama ..." I was the only one playing my own version of it over and over in my head for more than twenty years every time I thought of high school. That is what we do to ourselves. That is how we let other people affect us. We write our own script for our cast of characters. We fill in the blanks. And it's usually worst-case scenario. You actually have control over that right now, and you can choose the story you tell yourself and the story that will be told about you for years to come. The cast of characters near you will repeat whatever words you choose.

A Bad Outing to Church

After the accident with Sam, there were television live trucks on my lawn. It was the lead story on the TV and in the paper for several days. Sam stayed in the news as he had more surgeries and the town held more prayer vigils. During this time I stayed home, in my house, away from everyone who I was sure thought I was a terrible person. I was exhausted from crying and thinking and trying to make it not be real. I didn't know what the next minute, much less the next day, would bring. I was in a holding pattern. I built scenarios in my head where mothers told their children to stay away from me like I was some type of monster. I felt like the world was better off without me. The things

I conjured up about how other people were reacting were outrageous, but to me they were very real. A few days after the accident, I insisted that I needed to go to a prayer vigil for Sam. I needed to show people that I was a good person and that I was praying for him too. There had been several vigils, but this one was at "our" church. Yes, my coanchor and I went to the same church. I felt like I just had to be there. My husband said it was a bad idea, but I was adamant and thought it would be worse if I did not go.

***

I should introduce my new husband, Ben, here. After my divorce, I married the morning show weatherman (he would say meteorologist). That story is for a different book, what is important for this book is not his meteorology degree , but his other college degree. When I remarried, I had no idea that a husband with a psych degree would come in so handy. The accident with Sam happened one year into our marriage and some guys may have bailed. He was and still is the supporting character in my story who is instrumental in my ability to get through the tough times. THIS was no cakewalk for him. I was an irrational, emotional basket case who was not easy to deal with. I've asked him to add his tips for your support team later in the book.

***

Back to the church. My husband drove. We were careful to come in late after everyone was seated and we scooted into a pew in the back. The pew was to the right, only a few feet from the door. I still remember the scene vividly. I didn't make eye contact, but I could feel people staring at me. The church had a balcony. I was sure everyone above me was looking down on me, I could physically feel the weight of their glances. It was heavy and painful..I don't remember much of what was said or who I saw, but I stayed the whole time. When we left, I was in much worse shape than I had been before we went. That night, I was sure my life was over and that I would never feel OK in public again. I could not imagine a world in which I could be seen as anything other than the woman who ran over the baby with her car. My husband had been right. It was a bad idea to go.

I share this because you may want to make some bad decisions as well. I was fortunate that people around me knew better than me and tried to shield me from myself. He and others did more than I knew, intercepting calls and emails and creating a safe place. I'll share some tips from Ben at the end of this chapter. If you don't have a few people around to help you, then please know this: You have to create a filter to the outside world to protect yourself. The things our minds do to us in these situations are so messed up.

Fortunately for me, I had married a man with a psychology degree who knew I was gonna need that protection. Along with him, I closed my circle to a few close girlfriends, and I found a very good therapist. I still love my therapist to this day. Finding the right person for you is so important. One therapist I tried started our session by asking me to "find a happy place in my mind" and I just stood up from my chair and said – "I ran over my friends' baby's head – there is no 'expletive' happy place in here!" And I left. (Again – not a moment I am proud of). We are all different. That approach may work for some people, but I needed someone to give me something to work on. I needed a therapist to make me say all the crazy crap in my head out loud and then call me out on all the stuff that I was making up and help me find places for the stuff I was not. I highly recommend finding a trained therapist or at least a good friend who you can say things out loud too. You need these people. You need to say all that messed up stuff out loud to someone. Don't keep the dialogue running in your head. It has to come out.

So as we think about this crappy chapter in the book that is your life, there are a few filters to keep in mind as you make edits during this unfortunate plot twist. You need to take inventory of the characters (People), settings (Places) and themes (Words) in your story.

People

There are people who you will feel safe with, who you can talk openly around, and who you can share some of the crazy stuff that's going on in your head. That is a very small circle, a limited number of humans. Maybe one to three tops. That's it!! You do not have to explain this to everyone. I didn't even include my parents in that circle. It was too much for them and that would have been added stress for me.

There are people on the outside of that circle who care about you, who want to see you and know you are OK. Those people are safe to be around, but limit your time with them. Being around people is exhausting. You will end up trying to comfort them. You will struggle to find words to make them feel better. Quick hellos and hugs, or maybe a text or phone call is all that they need.

The rest of the world – literally everyone else in person, calling, or on social media –does not need to know what you are thinking and going through. This goes especially for those who are "in this with you" – they may need to be kept out of your circle for a while. You need to heal, they need to heal, and it is so much harder to do that together. My husband shielded me from so much pain. He got up early and hid the newspaper and didn't let me take some phone calls, or watch regular TV (preselected movies were OK for an escape – he would be sure they didn't have small children in perilous situations in them). If it were today, I am sure he would have taken my phone. Your brain can't keep replaying THIS and taking that beating. It needs a break.

As much as I wanted to go to the hospital and sit vigil at Sam's bedside with his mother, I realized after one visit (and a meltdown afterward) that it was too much for both of us. She needed to focus on him and her own survival. I was another piece of her pain. I wasn't helping. I prayed for their family and kept my distance.

Places

For a while there may be places you need to avoid. Sometimes I wasn't even aware of them until I was there. For me, the obvious places, like the cul-de-sac where the accident happened, triggered painful emotions. In the weeks and months that followed, I discovered the carpool line was a no-go. Too many kids and car tires. Parks had too many small kids who might get hurt at any moment. Then came parades! I was not ready for this one. Each television station has a float in local Christmas parades, and I didn't realize until I was riding on a float, rolling down the street with small children feet away from the tires, that I should not have been there. A giant wave of fear and anxiety hit me, my heart rate skyrocketed, I got that awful feeling in my spine and my gut and for the next hour I tried to manage the panic inside me as I smiled and waved.

Do some prework. Think about what places and situations THIS could make hard for you and then be kind to yourself. Skip them for a while. Let yourself heal.

Words

Filtering the words you hear and repeat, may be the most important filter for today's social media world. The words people say or write strangely may not be the actual words you see or hear. Your brain is not normal during this crappy chapter and has a mind of its own. It is like you have on headphones that filtered the words that your ears can hear. These magical noise-canceling headphones filter out all the good stuff and let only the negative words get in.

We Are Wired to Remember the Bad Stuff

After the accident with Sam, I received hundreds of emails from viewers who were supportive and loving and kind. I remember none of them. Not one comes to mind as I write this right now. I remember only the two that said that I must be a terrible person. I can still see where the words were on the screen. That is how we are wired. We don't remember the good stuff, just the bad.

Here is how this works. Someone might say, "Oh I am so sorry this happened. You are a wonderful human, and I can't believe you are going through this horrible time." That sounds fine in a normal brain. But in the middle of this crappy chapter – this is all you can hear: "HORRIBLE blab bla YOU bla bla bla." Then "HORRIBLE" replays even though they only said it once. It is so wrong, but it's real during THIS, so you need to shield yourself from too much of it.

I share all these scenarios to get you thinking. Depending on what your THIS is, it may be best to keep your circle small, ditch your mobile device, and have a friend monitor it, so you can give yourself a break. You need it.

I hope you have a few wonderful people around you to support you. If so, ask them to read this chapter. Let them help you. Even if you think you are tough, and think that you've got THIS. I am telling you that you don't. You need to let a few folks in. Your crappy chapter needs to have a cast of characters. Choose your characters wisely.

Relationship tip for you. (I didn't always do this well.) For those people who are genuinely trying to help you, you need to cut them some slack. They are just trying to figure out how to help you. They don't know how to get through THIS either. Here are some tips from my husband. Share these with your support people.

BEN'S TIPS

- Let the person talk, vent, verbalize their thoughts without interruption and without judgment.
- Engage the person in their own behavioral solutions. You can help them work on it; give feedback on their plan. What do they want to accomplish? How do they think a particular exercise, thought pattern, reaction, or behavior is going to help? Is that a realistic perception of the world around them? What assumptions is the person making about how the rest of the world will react or about how others think? It can be helpful to take note of

and point out ways in which the person's assumptions (or fears) may not match reality. But this can be very treacherous territory. It doesn't help the person going through all this crap to remind them that among other flaws (which they will no doubt be sensitive to, and fixated on, and which they may or may not actually have) they don't even see what's going on around them. Pointing that out can make them feel selfish, and guilty, and just way screwed up. So...

- Help the person realize that their reaction to this traumatic situation is normal. Racing thoughts? Normal. Guilt and shame? Normal.
- Empower them with their own recovery. Celebrate the victories
- Life will be different. Be honest and realistic. Sometimes trauma includes physical trauma. We simply cannot do some things the same way. Injuries and illnesses can't always be fixed. But life does not end. There is always a new challenge and a new frontier. Book suggestion: *The Obstacle Is the Way*, Ryan Holiday
- Embrace the change. They aren't the same person. But they might be a better, stronger person.
- This is tough. You may not be a part of their new story. It's not your deficiency or theirs. You can't will someone to recover, and you can't will

someone to have you be a part of their recovery. But this may be a once-in-a-lifetime opportunity for you to practice selflessness.

- You will be stressed too. You will need breaks.
- You won't always do or say the right thing. Focus on your good intentions to help. Ask for help yourself. Do your best. Don't try to hide it when you screw up or cover it up. Just be honest about it. And talk about how you might screw up from the beginning (and reiterate it from time to time). It can reinforce to the person that you can both roll with the punches. Ups and downs are a normal and necessary part of moving on.
- Help the person practice objective assessment of the world around them and their own behavior. "Hey, this is one of my freak out moments! Isn't it great that I noticed it?! Awesome. Now I remember that my strategy is to politely excuse myself and go cry in my car for ten minutes. Sweet!"
- The closer you are to the person, the tougher this will be. It's a crap ton of stress. It's exhausting. Remember that even though your stress is not anywhere near the other person's stress, that doesn't diminish its effect on you.
- You may not get thanked. You may feel underappreciated. In fact, you probably will. Find someone of your own to talk with.

- The stress from this doesn't end quickly. Nina writes about how much of your life big events can be, and how to think of them with a long-term perspective. I think of these events as having "resonant time," time where the trauma is still affecting someone's physical or mental state. That can be a long time, and it might feel like a long time for you to feel committed to someone else's recovery. But this is a rich part of your story too. Life can be long.

- You are not the hero. You can only be a guide. You should never take credit for the triumph of another person. It is great that you helped, but you did not get them through this. It's not your victory. It's most definitely not yours to hold against that person. If you try to make this yours, you will lose that person, you will lose the value of your effort and support, and you will lose your way. It's hard not to build up some resentment from time to time, especially when the person may lash out at you from time to time. You may have to distance yourself, and you must develop your own strategies to deal with feelings you will inevitably have. Don't pretend they won't occur. Don't think such feelings are abnormal or make you a bad person. Practice what you preach. Have a plan. Be objective. Understand that life is long and there's more to your story too.

CHAPTER 6:

This Is Just One Chapter – It's a Long Story

"What lies behind us and what lies before us are tiny matters compared to what lies within us."
– Ralph Waldo Emerson

his next coping tool is one that I didn't have for most of my life. I wish I had. I didn't learn this jewel of knowledge until I was about forty-five. This may be the best concept I can share with you as you work through THIS. It works for all ages, but if you are a college student, I sure hope you read this chapter even if you don't read this whole book. I think colleges should teach this your freshman year. Someone in academia could do this perspective concept much better than me, but here is how I see it.

Life is long. Yep, you heard me. All the quotes, books, and T-shirts with sayings about life is short, grab the ring, buy the shoes, make it sweet, dance in the rain, or whatever,…those are not necessarily wrong, but they are a bit misleading, and I would caution that they can be dangerous. I wish I had known how many plot twists and crazy chapters my life would turn out to have back when I was thinking my life was over at nineteen because I could no longer do gymnastics. Holy crap! That seems crazy now. That is such a small part of the life I have had now. I can't even put into words how real it felt at the time, and how overwhelmingly sad the thought that I felt it was over, makes me now. It was so all encompassing at nineteen, it was very real, but I now have a different perspective. I can do the math and see it becomes a small percentage of my life. I have actual data that I can reference. I can see that my life 'as I knew it' was over because my life experience at nineteen years was mostly gymnastics. I just didn't realize that my life story was a thick book and that there would be so many more chapters and characters and highs and lows and plot twists.

The best way to explain my 'Life is Long' concept is to share it with you the same way I learned it and then let you do it for yourself. So here is a *love story* in the middle of this book about tragedies. Stick with me – it makes a point.

A Love Story

Disclosure: My husband insists that he is OK with this story – partly because he was once young and head over heels in love too and partly because he is secure in our marriage and knows I think he's sexy and smart and that he makes the best scrambled eggs. That is not a euphemism – just talking about eggs people, get your head out of the gutter.

I met Chris the summer after my sophomore year of college. My parents were living in Jacksonville, Florida, and I went home for the summer. We met in the local gym where a lot of the Navy pilots from NAS JAX worked out. I'm no dummy. I chose that gym wisely. Chris had graduated from the Naval Academy, and he was the best-looking one of the bunch. He had beautiful blue eyes that seemed so kind. Within weeks I had decided he was the kindest, most handsome man I had ever met. We dated that summer and fell head over heels in love. What followed were months in which we made some amazing memories. When he was sent to Maine for training, I drove with him from Florida to Maine and for a month we lived in a small house on a tiny island that had only a few houses on it. We ate lobster and explored the coast. Maine was beautiful. He was beautiful. All my thoughts that summer had the word beautiful in them, and the memories seem magical. Later, during my junior year at LSU, Chris got stationed in Rota, Spain. He wrote me love letters in his beautiful handwriting. (Stay with me, I know you are dealing with THIS, but this story is making a point.) We had been together about two years and we started to think about our future. At some point, my mind started playing out what I thought our future would look like. You see, I had grown up a Navy brat, and we moved a lot, so I started filling in the blanks of a future with Chris with things that were not so beautiful. I envisioned moves to new towns, lots of crying babies, and large chunks of time when my would-be husband would be overseas. So, while Chris was in Spain, I decided I had no idea where my life was going yet, but I did not want a house full of his beautiful children with a white picket fence and I did not want to spend my life waiting for him to come home. I could see no way that he could do the job he loved, flying for the Navy, and I could have my own career. So – I wrote him a long heartfelt breakup letter, sent it to him in Spain, and ended it. (there was no Facetime back them. I could not even call him) We both were crushed in our own ways. The next thing I heard about Chris was that he had taken an assignment to Reykjavik, Iceland. I was sure he did so to get as far away from me on the planet as he could get.

So why am I telling you this? That magical two years seemed like my whole life at the time and that decision seemed like a make or break moment. If I didn't make the right decision, everything would be ruined. In fact, later in my life, when things would go wrong, I would revisit that decision and think…if I had just married Chris then life may have been perfect. Hey – maybe on Earth 2 that is what my doppelgänger did, and she has six kids and has never worked a day in her life. Maybe she plays tennis at the club, and has a flat stomach and perfect clothes for every occasion.

Back to reality on this earth, even with all the pain and failures and messes in my life, I wouldn't trade it. The tough stuff makes us who we are. I have a great husband who really gets me. We have this blended family with college kids that I love more than I can even put in words. I have work friends that I met even when I didn't want to go to work some days, and cycling friends I met during Alzheimer's charity rides when my dad was dying from that disease. So many people who have come into my life story in good times and bad times have changed me in some way. Just doing the mental gymnastics to think about all of their influences helps me. But what really helped me put things in perspective was reconnecting with Chris twenty-five years later. And it's not what you think. He was successful and still handsome with those beautiful, kind blue eyes.

Chris and I reconnected through Facebook. He was living in Dallas. So during my next work trip to Dallas, we arranged to have dinner. (Yes, I told my husband – that is not where this story is going; get your mind out of the gutter.) We met at a restaurant. At first it was awkward, but after only a few minutes, it was so easy to connect. The conversation was engaging. Like me, he had been married and had children and then divorced. We shared pictures of our kids and talked about where life had taken us. We talked for hours until the restaurant closed. Then we found a bar and talked until last call. The bartender kicked us out. We still had a ton of catching up to do, but more than that, we truly cared about each other's stories. As we said goodbye, I remember thinking, I feel love for this man and I really don't even know him. It seemed bizarre that I could have such a strong emotion. It was not like the love I have for my husband, but it felt like much more than a friendship.

We stayed in touch. Months later, I was back in Dallas for work, and we had dinner again. That is when I learned this concept I call "Life Is Long."

Chris and I talked about how easy it was to talk and how much we cared about each other's lives. He said he thought he knew why. It was not just the magical memories we shared; it was the time in which those memories were formed. At that time, in our lives, those two years were a large percentage of our entire lives. Those months were a big part of our life experience, and even more so, they were the majority of what we knew about love. He wrote it out on a piece of paper for me. I still have it in his handwriting and I share it with you now. Thinking of life this way was mind-altering for me.

The older you get, the smaller each segment of your life is compared to the whole of your life. Each day, week, month, year, the percentages adjust as we go through life. It looks like this:

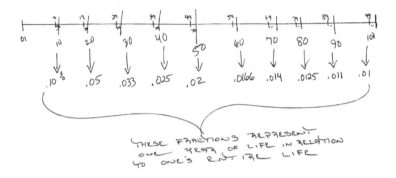

When you are ten years old, that year of your life is one-tenth of our whole life. When you are fifty, a year is one-fiftieth, which is a much smaller figure for the same 365 days. As you get older, each year becomes a smaller percentage of your whole life. This is why life seems to keep moving faster as you get older. Our timelines adjust each day. This concept got me thinking about when I was a kid, when I first fell in love, my time in school, and all those years parenting.

A Ten-Year-Old Summer

Think about when you were ten years old, and the summers felt like they went on forever. If you are in your thirties or forties now, I bet the summers seem to fly by. Well if you do the math, that summer (three months), at age ten, is 2.5 percent of your whole life as you know it at that point. The more you live, the smaller that fraction becomes.

If we look at summer as a special segment of 'kid time' the difference increases. Summers for kids have more hours for them to interact with friends. Over a twelve-week summer, a kid may average 4 hours a day with friends, that's 28 hours a week, which gives a kid 336 hours of super fun preteen summertime. Throw in a summer camp, and it's more!

We can also break the percentage down further if we only count when a person is old enough to have interpersonal relationships. Some estimate we develop that ability at about age five. So if we only count from age five to ten, then one summer is much more than 10 percent.

If you play with some math, you will find that a summer when you are ten-years-old equals about the same percentage of your life experience as a full year does when you are forty!

A Summer When You Are Forty

At age forty, one summer makes up less than 1 percent your life and the time is not all yours. A forty-year-old with a job and kids may have a nine-hour workday, seven hours of sleep (on a good night), and an hour of getting ready and commuting. Then you have the hours taken up by jobs/chores/carpools/watching kids' athletic events and workouts. If it's a very demanding job, or more than two kids, or you have a parent to care for, then an adult summer, even with two weeks of vacation, and only eight-hour workdays leaves you very little time left to binge watch Netflix.

High School and College

When you are in high school or college, that four-year span of your life can seem long. Some of us wanted to just get through them and others wanted them to last forever. Sometimes a person's THIS happens in high school or college, and it rocks their world so much they become anxious, depressed, or suicidal. If you do the math on those years, you can see why. They are experiencing those years of their life as a HUGE percentage of what they know of life. It is their perspective. If they do the math, they will find it's actually a small percentage of their entire life. If they use the "Life is Long" concept, they may grasp the bigger picture. Here's the math around high school and college.

For this example, let's start with someone who is fifteen years old. For the four years of high school, we will count every hour of every day (waking, nonwaking, in school, at work). Freshman year is one-fifteenth of a fifteen-year-olds' lives. By the end of their freshman year, 6.7 percent of their life has been spent in high school. Each school year after, that high school percentage jumps up.

- At age sixteen, high school is two-sixteenths of their life, so by the end of sophomore year that's 12.5 percent.
- At age seventeen, high school is three-seventeenths of their life, so by the end of junior year that's 17.6 percent.
- At age eighteen, high school is four-eighteenths of their life, so by the end of their senior year, that's 22.2 percent.

If a person goes straight to college out of high school, the math continues like this.

Their freshman year in college at age nineteen is one-nineteenth or 5.3 percent of their life. Each year their college percentage jumps up.

- At age twenty, college becomes two-twentieths, or 10 percent, of their life.
- At age twenty-one, college becomes three-twenty-firsts, about 14.3 percent of their life.
- At age twenty-two, when they graduate, the college experience has become four-twenty-seconds, or 18.2 percent of their life.

Before we move on from these school examples of 'Life is Long' – middle school can be a tough time for some kids and this math is eye-opening. If middle school for you was three years long, and you were fourteen when it ended, your middle school experience was about 21.4 percent of your entire life to that point. That's a lot!

Adulting

Life seems to fly by when we are adulting. Time is money when we are working and raising kids. It is easy to see why when we compare that four-year span of college to a four-year span of your life when you are working and parenting.

We will use ages forty-one to forty-five for this example. For many people, those are some of the most active and prime-earning years of your working life. Those same years you may be parenting your kids through some of their defining moments in life – ages twelve to sixteen. That four-year span of your life in your forties that is chock-full of super-important stuff equals 8.9 percent of your life to that point. That is about the same percentage of the one-year span that was sixth grade. That was 8.3 percent.

Yes, the math can work against us. Keep this in mind when you spend time with your kids. One year of your life at age forty is an underwhelming 2.5 percent of your life experience. That same year for your ten-year-old is 10 percent of their life experience.

My Lifetime in a Timeline

With this new thinking, I built my own timeline and wanted to do some math to put the chapters of my life into perspective. If I live to one hundred (wishful thinking and I need to start eating better), then what percentage would my gymnastics training be, or my news career, or my time in tech equal? What percentage was I a mom with kids at home?

What percentage of my life were the men in my life story? Here is how the math helps me put my life in perspective.

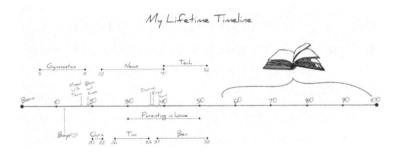

My Math Facts

Being a mom, at home with kids was twenty years of my life, from age thirty to fifty.

- 40 percent when they all went away to college
- 20 percent of my life if I live to age one hundred

Fun Fact: When I was forty years old and was busy parenting kids ages eight, nine, and ten. That parenting experience was 25 percent of my life. That twenty years is about the same percentage as my four-year high school experience was at the time.

By the time I was fifty, I had had at least one child under my roof for twenty years. Parenting represented about 40 percent of my life experience. By the time all of my kids left the house for college, I had been a parent for a much larger percentage of my life than I'd been a gymnast (40 percent parenting compared to 28 percent gymnastics). That gives perspective to the nineteen-year-old me who thought my life was over when I could no longer do gymnastics. What I felt in college was real, but the data alters my view of that life experience. "Life Is Long."

Back to Love

Of course I did the math to figure out the leading men in my life. There were a few other loves along the way, but I wanted to figure out why I still felt a kind of love for Chris after all these years. If you had young love then this may resonate with you. Here is the breakdown of my leading men.

Chris: We dated for two years. When we broke up, I was twenty-two. That means he was in 9.1 percent of my life experience at that point. But if I only count from age 12 when I realized I "liked boys in new ways" that becomes about 20 percent of my romantic life experience. Those short two years were one-fifth of all I knew. No wonder they stuck with me.

Husband 1/Tim: My first husband and I dated and were married for a total of ten years when we divorced. I was thirty-five years old when we split up, so that means he was in 28.6 percent of my life when we split. If I count from age twelve, that becomes 43.5 percent of my romantic life experience. No wonder divorce felt like my life would never be the same! Now that I'm at fifty-two, he is 19 percent, and when I am one hundred and look back on it, Tim will be 10 percent.

Ben: Ben and I have been together for about fifteen years as I write this. At age fifty-two he is 28.8 percent of my life and a solid 38 percent of my romantically aware life. Of course I wanted to figure out how old I would be when his percentages surpass the others. I am almost there. At age fifty-six, the percentage of my romantic life experience with Ben will finally surpass the percentage of my romantic life experience with my first husband. Those eighteen years of marriage will equal the 10 years of my first marriage.

Timeline Your Life Story

I suggest you create your own 'Life Is Long' Timeline. Here is a blank lifespan to help you get started. Put in the milestones, activities, careers, people, and places that tell your life story. Fill it out and do some math. If you are not good at math, find a friend who is. (Thank you to Ben and my son Jake for helping me with mine)

Lifetime Timeline

Born 10 20 30 40 50 60 70 80 90 100

Ideas for your Lifetime Timeline

- Events / Milestones
- Sports / Activities
- Locations / Moves to new towns
- Relationships
- Jobs / Careers
- Kids / Family
- "THIS"

I am not sure why this visual representation of my story speaks to me in the way that it does. Somehow looking at my life this way eases my anxiety. Maybe it's because I can see the accomplishments and the failures together. Maybe it's because I can see that the really big chunks of time were not for nothing. Some great things happened during those years too. Part of the reason this visual aid helps me is because I can see the blank space ahead.

Blank Pages

I like the thought of the blank pages. I like the thought of the next chapters unwritten, all of those empty pages. I can choose what to write there. I could sell everything tomorrow, buy an RV and drive around the country; maybe I pick up odd jobs along the way, and meet people, and hike, and cycle. I could decide to learn to paint and dive into the local art scene, open my own gallery in a few years, and wear outrageous clothing that I can't wear in my corporate job. I could stay in my corporate job and add a line on that chart to show how much money I make, and chart my wealth, and someday add mile markers to show the charities and the difference that I make with that money. For now, I've decided to fill some of that blank space writing this book. There are an infinite number of settings, characters, and stories that I could choose to populate that empty space with.

So hopefully you see it now. That "Life Is Long' and having that perspective can ease your thinking around "everything is ruined." You get to write the part of your story that comes after THIS.

Tattoos

As you think about the concept that "Life Is Long" and the percentage of your life that THIS event occupies, I just want to share my thoughts on tattoos. And for the record, I am tattoo agnostic, neither pro-tattoo nor anti-tattoo.

Tattoos often accompany these crappy chapters or defining moments. At a point in time THIS can feel like your whole life. We often want to own THIS, shout it from the rooftop because it is our whole world right now. Many people get tattoos to mark the highs and lows, to show these pivotal moments or milestones in their lives. I personally don't have any at the writing of this book, but if I think about my own milestones, I could have some fun ones: Olympic rings, with a line through them, an LSU tiger, a little Emmy statue, the word "Sam," the stock symbol for my company. I can picture them all.

My friend Jaclyn once told me there should be a wait period for tattoos. She had never had one until her mom died when she was in her thirties. She was very close to her mother, and when her mother became ill, Jaclyn became her caregiver. When her mother passed, it was a crushing and defining event in Jaclyn's life. She wanted to hold on to everything she could about her mom. So about a week after her death, she got a tattoo on her right forearm of a heart and the word *Mom*. She won't say she regrets it and doesn't cover it up, but she did say that there should be a large sign in the tattoo shop that reads, "We check life event registries; mandatory six-month wait period for family deaths." It's sort of like buying a gun on impulse, maybe you should have to wait 'til the emotion is not so overwhelming. Years later she got another tattoo. This one she spent time thinking about and designing. Talking about that new piece of artwork makes her feel confident and proud.

There is a super smart author who wrote two really great books. His name is Ryan Holiday, author of *The Obstacle Is the Way* and *Ego Is the Enemy*. I don't know him, but I highly recommend his books. I read somewhere that Ryan Holiday has those two book titles, his mantras, written on his arms. Upon hearing this, the first thing I thought was, *How old is this guy?* I actually looked up his age. He's young. He was born in 1987! I thought maybe I should reach out to him and tell him my concept about life being long. He's super smart, and these books are so good. I think he needs to leave space for more. 'Life is Long' and he is so talented. I am worried he is going to run out of skin.

I also thought about "Life Is Long" when I saw Adam Levine take off his shirt during his Super Bowl halftime show in 2019. Like other women watching, I appreciated his physique. Then I started reading the tattoos and thought, *There must be emotional meanings in all of his ink. He's capturing his meaningful memories with these tattoos. I am worried he's going to run out of skin.* Levine is so talented, I wanted to contact him somehow and tell him to choose carefully, save some space, because "Life is Long'.

We have played a game with our kids since they were little. Usually we would play it on the way home from the beach when we were are all sandy and happy and a little silly. On the beach, people usually don't cover up much skin, so you often see everyone's tattoo artwork on display. The game goes like this. One of us would say, "Today's the day! We are all going to go straight downtown to get tattoos. What are you getting?" Everyone has to choose a tattoo design during the car ride and decide by the time we got home. Through the years this has been a fun time to think of our favorite things, our defining moments, and later, to laugh about our younger selves.

Between our three kids, there would be tattoos of a red Power Ranger, a my little pony, the symbol for pi, an awesome Minecraft thing going up a leg, a frog, grandparents' names, an infinity loop with a heart, the atomic symbol for water, and so many more. The list is a roadmap of each person's past, a visual representation of their lives and the things they are passionate about. At seventeen, my son Jake, a baseball player, designed an amazing tattoo that he was sure he would get near the scar left from the Tommy John surgery he had to repair his injured throwing arm. He was going to rehab his arm back, throw one hundred miles per hour, and when he hit that goal, he was going to have the scar made into the smiling mouth of a face and have some flames up his arms. I think somewhere he also had the names of each of his grandparents written very tiny in the design. It was cool.

We made a deal with our kids when they were in high school. We would pay for college, but there were a few conditions. One of those was no tattoos while you are still in school, and we meant it. No artwork 'til you graduate. Some may think this is a silly thing to make such a big deal about, but I wanted college to be the years when they were figuring out who they were. Away from their parents, they could have their own political views, learn what love is, use their brains, and decide on their own what they think is right and wrong. I wanted them to have a blank slate for their passions to change. There is so much that happens in those years between eighteen and twenty-two, so many emotions and changes, and I think a clean slate gives them license to make those changes unencumbered. After that, if they want to get some artwork on their body that lasts for their entire long life then that's up to them.

So bottom line: if THIS is something you want literally written on your body, keep in mind that people will ask you about it. You will have to tell the story over and over. If you don't want THIS to define you, you may want to choose another way to embrace it.

CHAPTER 7:

You Can't Go Back
for a Rewrite

"If you are depressed you are living in the past.
If you are anxious you are living in the future.
If you are at peace you are living in the present."
— Lao Tzu

A t this point, you are figuring out where to put THIS in your head. You know you need to set up some filters, and I hope you are getting some perspective that life is long. The next thing to do is to think forward.

With your new added perspective you can now think of this THIS as the pages of a crappy chapter that you are trying to get past. As much as you would like to rip these pages out, you can't, and your story is still unfolding, moving forward. There are an infinite number of possibilities for where it will go. Your best bet for making it to a chapter that you like is to figure out what that chapter might look like. What is it that you want for your life? Randomly waiting and hoping for something to unfold to get you out of this sludge should not be your plan. Hope is not a strategy. No one knows who said that quote first, but it is true for our story. You need to decide you want to get past THIS and actively start thinking about what's next.

You Before THIS and You After

I had a good friend who was in the hospital a few years ago. Our kids were teenagers and we were both working moms with pretty stressful jobs. It was the holidays, and she and her family had rented a beach house. This beautiful (did I mention she was beautiful) perfectly healthy woman in her forties started feeling odd the day after Christmas and ended up in the hospital with a collapsed lung. The doctors had to do an emergency surgery. They intubated her and knocked out a veneer then shoved tubes in her side to save her life. She woke up with stitched up holes in her side and missing a front tooth. She wouldn't let anyone come visit her except her family and me. When I saw her she was distraught, drugged up, and angry. She said, "I look like a gunshot victim who was dragged from homeless shelter." (Please remember that she was drugged up, so we are going to let the very inappropriate comment about toothless homeless people slide this time.) For the first two days after her emergency surgery, she vented. She was sad and afraid that she would never be able to do physical things again without worrying she would collapse and die. She kept returning to "why me?" in each discussion. On day three when I went to visit and take her the latest People magazine, she started again with the "why me?" I said something that day that changed her thinking. I didn't realize how important the words I chose that day were until years later when we were talking and she said my words made her think differently. I had said something like, "Can we please move on now? This is your reality. There was a you before this and there will be a you after this and lots of stuff you can do. Can we start thinking about the 'you after this'? Let's figure that out."

That is what you have to do at some point. You have to start figuring out what's next. This crappy chapter is just that. It is a chapter in your long life. I hope you can see that now. There was a you before THIS and you cannot go back to being that person. There has been too much character development since THIS rocked your world. THIS has changed you, and the you after THIS will be different.

Timing Your Next Step

The timing of this next step is a tough one. I know people who get stuck fighting against change. They don't want to be different than they used to be. They were happy. They liked the previous version of themselves. We all know people like this. People stuck in their problems, defined by their situation, unable to move forward. It is difficult. You see this a lot with divorce. One spouse unwilling to let go of the dream and clinging to the hope that somehow it is going to go back to how it was, and a Christmas morning with everyone around the tree. You also see a different version of this after the death of a loved one. You find people who don't want to let go of that person, don't want to imagine a life without them. It hurts too much to think about it so they become workaholics or dive into something else. They distract themselves with anything that takes up their time because they just can't move forward. It's too hard. I get it. This is not an easy step. I never said this was easy, but life is going to keep moving forward with or without you, so it is necessary.

You have to make up your mind that you are ready to move forward. If you really want to get THIS to stop taking up so much space in your brain and you want to stop the sludge that is filling your soul, you have to decide you are going to move away from it. You've got to pick a path and start down it. If you don't then THIS will define you. You are the only one who can decide that this crappy chapter is just that, a chapter in your life, not your whole life. Once you start thinking of it as one chapter, then you can start thinking about the next chapter. There will be a new you after this and you will need to start moving in that direction.

The Old You – Is Gone

A new you. Yes, I hate to tell you but the old you is gone. The "you" before this crappy chapter, the person that you so desperately want to go back and be again, just isn't real. You have changed. The good news is, you get to keep all the great things about that old you that you loved. Make a list of them. Your favorite foods, your favorite things to do, your favorite movies. They all get to come with you into the next chapter. Those deep-seated values that you don't want to change, those can come too. In this new chapter, you will know things you did not know before and feel differently about things than you may have before. That's OK. That's part of a lifetime of learning and growing. You will bring those with you.

This new chapter may have many of the same characters and settings. Some of them may not make the edit. Still, your story will go on without them.

People: There may be people who don't make the edit. If so, then that person may have been in your story for only a short time for character development. You likely learned from them. Good or bad, all that learning comes with you. You can think of it like you do an old boyfriend. Having him in your earlier chapters, you learned what you liked about a partner and what you didn't. You saw new places and you experienced all sorts of things with this person. Those things you liked, the places and the experiences, come with you. The person does not. That person is actually writing their own story and it is about them – not you. I know – shocker!

Places: There may be places that don't make the edit. If so, then that place may have only been a setting for your story for a short while. You will move on to new place and be able to compare it to that last place. Might be better, might be worse, but now you will know the difference. Maybe it is a workplace. When you are fired from a job, it can be so jarring. I thought the newsroom I worked in and the way we interacted with each other was perfect. When I was fired and went to a new newsroom, I could not believe how well everyone got along and how good a hard news day could be even in the most stressful situations. My old TV station didn't make the edit in my life, but the experience of it helped form my next chapter. I would have never known it could be different without the first one.

Thoughts: This will be different for sure. The way you think will be different in the next chapter. The main character has gone through something that can't be undone. If you used to think that you had a plan and nothing was going to change that, then you now know better. If you thought that bad things didn't happen to good people and the world was your oyster. You may be a bit jaded and less carefree. On the other hand you now know that THIS won't kill you. You are reading this book, so you've already proven that. This new thinking all comes with you too. Your new knowledge will be important to the main character (you) in the next chapter. You have developed some life skills that you may not have known you needed. But you've got them now.

You are becoming the next version of yourself. You are writing your story. No one else has as much power as you do to form this next chapter, to choose the words, the characters, and the setting.

Some Thoughts on Your Story and God

If you are trying to fit THIS into your religious beliefs, these next few paragraphs are for you. During events in my life when I went from a super high moment to a crushing low, I did a lot of the why-would-God-do-this-to-me kind of thinking. It goes something like this: "I am a good person. I have done nice things for others. I have prayed. I am not perfect, but why would God do this to me." I am guessing you may have a similar internal rant going on in your head.

During a horrible event in your life, people tell you, "God has a plan for you" or "Everything happens for a reason" or "This is part of God's plan for you." They are all well-meaning, but when you are in the middle of THIS and it's your ruined plan – it is really hard to see how THIS could be part of anyone's plan. I struggled. I was irrational and argumentative. I write this with that tone because I am guessing you might be as well. So take this how you want to. This is my nondenominational advice for you during THIS. I believe that during THIS, you have license to believe or change your beliefs in any way you need to, to get through THIS.

So back to "God has a plan." If you are trying to figure out if there is some master plan, some scenarios are easier to buy into than others. Maybe if you didn't get into the college you wanted - your soul mate is at the other school where you will end up. Or maybe if you got fired, your next big opportunity is at the next company that hires you. Those might be part of some master plan someone could sell you. There are some life events in which God's plan is a harder sell. How about the athlete who spent his whole life training to someday be in the Super Bowl…then drops the touchdown pass. Did God like the other team more? Or the expectant mother who sets up a beautiful nursery with all the baby shower gifts her friends and family gave her and posts pictures on Facebook to share her joy as she heads to the hospital…then her perfect, beautiful child dies within hours of being born. I am sorry. It is tough to buy that that is part of some plan. In my case, I searched long and hard to figure out how God could possibly make a plan to have my friend's beautiful baby boy end up under the tire of my car. I came to the conclusion, if that was His plan, then that's one sick god. (Yes, I just said it.) After the accident with Sam, I said a lot of things.

My pastor came over to the house often. He was calming and scholarly. We talked and he brought me books. I like to find meaning in books, and I devoured them all. I read some more than once. I struggled, so he expanded my thinking past traditional religion. I decided I might be Buddhist or maybe Lakota Indian (earth, wind, rain). The more books he brought, the more I searched. I prayed hard sometimes, then stopped praying at times, then stopped going to church altogether for a while. For many years, I chose to spend Sunday mornings walking the beach with my children. We would talk about silly things that made us happy and big meaningful things that touched on faith. We called it "church of the beach." Over time, I noticed many of the same people were on the beach each Sunday. For years it was our place for faith. Sometimes, we would pass other regulars walking towards the beach as we left. With a wave and a smile we would say "We went to early service today. It was great". Faith is a journey, and I have found that many people who go through THIS are on a similar journey. And that's OK!

Back to the more traditional God that many of you may be praying to, the Father, Son, and Holy Ghost that people refer to when they say they are praying for you during THIS. When I think about the concept "Life is Long" and try to fit in how God with a capital G fits into our story writing, here is one way you can think of it. God has a rough draft, a version 1! Everyone knows that all great stories have had to go through edits, revisions, and rewrites. In great stories, the setting, characters, conflict, plot and theme evolve. A plot twist can take our whole cast of characters in new directions.

The bottom line: It's your story and somehow you have to make this really horrible chapter of your life segue into the next one. If you are praying and waiting for God to do your story revisions, I don't think he does them. I think he gave you everything you need to create a really great story for yourself and he is not responsible for everyone's edits. There are no religious constraints on how you get past THIS. You have to take THIS plot twist, use what you've got, and get yourself to the next chapter.

Note:

There are some people who get stuck in their crappy chapter, who cannot get past the my-life-is-ruined mindset. They are waiting for some divine intervention to make it all better or for it to all magically be OK. Some people get stuck in the if-I-could-only-go-back-and-do-it again mode or the THIS-has-ruined-my-life-mode. That thinking is not sustainable. It is destructive, and it can lead to really dark thoughts and a very bleak future. If you are there, please don't skip the next chapter. The next chapter is important, because THIS is not the end.

CHAPTER 8:

Don't Let THIS Be 'The End'

"Though no one can go back and make a brand-new start, anyone can start from now and make a brand-new ending."
– Carl Bard

When I said that choosing to get out of this crappy chapter was tough, for some, that may be an understatement. If your THIS was bigger than losing the big game or losing your great job, you may feel like there is no way out. I have been there, and it scares me to think how close I came to "The End." It makes me sad now, but I am going to share my scary chapter because some of you need to know you'll be ok.

A few weeks after the accident with Sam I was lying on my back in my bedroom, just flopped on the carpeted floor. I am not sure how I got there or why. I remember lying there staring at the ceiling. I wasn't crying. I wasn't tired. I wasn't…anything. I remember thinking, this is odd – I don't feel…anything. I had been overwhelmed with emotions for days. I was so sad. I cried for Sam, for me, for his mom, for our kids, and for just everything. Everything was just so awful. Any time someone mentioned the accident or even looked at me and said, "How are you," I replayed the horror of the scene in my head. The adrenaline would rush through my veins and all the chemicals would flood my brain like it was happening right then.

Have you ever woken up from a really scary dream, your heart racing, and you're in a state of panic? You try to get your bearings, you sit up, and try to make sense of it. Then you finally calm down because you realize it's not real. But it seemed so real. Well, that's what THIS can do over and over all day and all night. But you never get to a point that the situation is not real no matter how hard you try.

So, why didn't I feel anything at this moment on the floor? It was still all very real and sweet little Sam was still barely alive and fighting for his life. Not much had changed, but I couldn't cry, the horror was gone, I didn't even feel anxious or scared. I laid there on the floor of my bedroom, all alone, and tried to get upset. I felt… nothing.

I couldn't understand it. It was like nothing I could explain. I thought, *Maybe I'm empty, maybe after a while your body physically runs out of emotions and tears and is just done*. I was a carcass. I laid on the floor, fascinated with this thought. I was a shell of myself without emotions. I looked down at my arm and thought *I could chop that arm off right now and I bet I couldn't even feel it*. I stared at it. I could move my hand; it wasn't numb. I just knew it would be like cutting into a thick piece of steak on a plate, it just wouldn't hurt. I actually pinched it – nothing. I was thinking about going and getting a knife to poke at it to test my theory when my husband walked in and said – "What are you doing on the floor." I told him, "I think I ran out of feelings. I think that I could chop my arm off and I wouldn't feel it".

Later he would tell me that that kinda freaked him out and he hid all the sharp objects in the house.

Here's some information from psychology experts about that: It's called *emotional numbness*:

EMOTIONAL NUMBNESS
- Part of the numbing response can come from the body and mind's self-protective efforts in the face of overwhelming emotions.
- Trauma leaves its imprint on the brain and greater brain activity in parts of the prefrontal cortex.

- The mind returns over and over to the upsetting memory, almost as if on a loop. It's like the brain is trying to make sense of the experience, or figure out if we should have responded differently.
- A flashback occurs when the trauma memory gets cued and makes it feel as if the trauma is happening all over again.
- Crying is associated with the parasympathetic nervous system, which calms the mind and body. Crying is one way the nervous system comes down from the fight-or-flight response.
- The nervous system has taken a major shock, and even while we are sleeping the brain continues to process the event.
- When the nervous system has had a terrifying shock, it doesn't immediately settle down. It's going to be turned up for a while, alert for the possibility of further danger.
- Researchers are still exploring the precise biology, chemistry, and brain changes that cause and are associated with this numbness.

Crazy Person Walking

More days went by and Sam was still alive. The whole town was praying for him, and there were still vigils and news stories – although the news trucks had left the front yard and moved on to other news stories. Soon, I got the courage to put on sweats and a baseball cap and go for a walk outside. I used to walk a few miles every day, and I decided I needed some fresh air and exercise might help clear the sludge, so I ventured out. We lived in a neighborhood near a county park. I did fine for a while. I walked and tried to think of different things, anything but the accident. I didn't walk down the street where it happened. I went the other way, kept my head down and didn't make eye contact with anyone. I was doing OK.

Then I turned onto the one busy road that led to the park entrance. I was on the walking path next to the road. It was not a sidewalk, but more like a biking and walking path right next to the road. A few cars sped by – no one seemed to noticed me. I was safe in my big sweatshirt and baseball cap, but my mind went to a dangerous place. I thought, "What if I just step in front of the next car that is going by? It would all be over so fast. What would that feel like? Would I feel anything? Probably not, I was empty. It would just all … end. This would be over. I wondered, how would that play out? I thought, *My family will be sad, but my new husband is great, and he is strong enough to handle it and he will help everyone else too. The kids have two dads now and grandparents in town. They will make it. They don't need a crazy, sad mom anyway.* It would be a sad story they told. My mom and dad and brothers and sister would be sad of course. My brother's church friends were praying for me, and they would all pray for him. My sister's husband would help her deal with it. My oldest brother was busy with his own kids and grandkids by this point. I figured he wouldn't have much time to be too sad. Then there was our community, the one that voted me Charleston's favorite news anchor. They would talk about it. It would be in the papers and it would be the chatter in the carpool lines and at water coolers. It would be a few additional lines to the evening news story that would roll through the teleprompter for my friends and coworkers to read. It would make this tragic story that much more compelling so ratings would go up even more. Yep, someone would make money off it. I thought about my coanchor and friend, it might help him. He would not have to ever sit next to me again, and he would have one less woman to worry about. His wife was going through what I was and more – overwhelming to even think about how much more. She had it worse than me. She was sitting in a hospital next to her baby. She probably hated me, but I couldn't even think about that yet. Yes, my coanchor could use one less person to have to take care of. It would be better if I was gone.

Then I thought about the driver of the car. *Well CRAP. I can't step in front of a car. If I do, then they are going to feel like I feel now.* They don't deserve to become the person who ran over the news anchor any more than I deserved to become the news anchor who ran over the baby. I can't pass this nightmare and pain on to them. That's a horrible thing to do. A few more cars went by, and I looked at the people driving, imagining their lives, imagining how they would react when they hit me, how they would pull over and jump out of the car horrified, and how gross it might look. What would they do? How would they lose it? Would they become like me in the days that followed? How would it replay in their minds over and over? Then...I snapped out of it. I thought. This is crazy, I am crazy. Wow! I seriously just thought out all of those deranged scenarios . That's so disturbed. I may actually be losing my mind – maybe I am.

I think I walked about three miles that day. I don't know. I just know I was gone a long time. My husband was worried that I had been gone so long. When I got back I wrote in my journal. That journal entry is even more alarming than the short version I just shared. I was pretty sure I was coming unhinged and that THIS was somehow the end.

I share my darkest moments because you may have some crazy dark thoughts as well, and you need to know that you are still normal. Your brain is trying to work through this, but it's not damaged beyond repair. It is temporary. You also need to know that some of the work to get through THIS, you can't do alone. If you are having dark, disturbing thoughts, you need to get some help. I had a husband with a psych degree, and we found a great therapist who worked with me. It was work for all of us. I had a very difficult time seeing past THIS. It seemed impossible at the time, and I resisted letting anyone in. Now that I am years past it, I am so thankful I did. Your future self, in the chapters ahead, needs you to be courageous and ask for help. You can get through THIS. Finding someone to help you is important. Do it, you are worth it.

Jimmy Stewart Jumped, It Was a Wonderful Life

If you think about it, speaking openly about suicide is not so taboo. We do it every year at Christmas time when we all tune in to watch Jimmy Stewart play George Bailey in *It's a Wonderful Life*. For you and me, our stories may be a little darker than it played out for George Bailey, but it's the same story. We can't figure out a scenario where things get better. . George Bailey could see no way out of his very public predicament (and apparently didn't know that insurance companies don't pay out for suicides) so he jumped off a bridge. In this magical movie, he gets to see the world without him and how his life story affected the life stories of his cast of characters. We are not in a movie. In real life our supporting characters may not be so clear-cut and the magical happy ending isn't so obvious The point is, some of us in the middle of THIS, just like George Bailey, are so caught up in THIS that we can't imagine the next chapters of our life story as anything but sad.

This defeated thinking hit me several times over the years. After the accident with Sam, my therapist encouraged me to own my story. I realized that I needed to handle things on my own terms somehow. I needed some control. To get that, we decided that I had to go back on the air with my coanchor. I needed to do that for me, and I thought we (my coanchor and I) needed to show our viewers that we were OK and that THIS had not broken us. My therapist and I came up with a plan. I would go back on the air for one year. I would be the supporting partner my coanchor needed while he took care of his family. If he needed to step away from work for his family, I would be there to handle things at work. I would do this for a year and then I could leave after that if I wanted to, on my own terms, head held high.

Back on the Air – A One-Year Sentence

My coanchor and I met to discuss the idea first. It was difficult to be around each other because it brought up so much emotion. We sat on his dock and I remember thinking that it felt like we were somehow stuck in a tragic news story. One of those 45 second stories that we would report and then segue to a more cheerful topic. There was no moving on from this one. Sitting on that doc, I thought we might only last a few weeks on the air, but we had to at least try.

At this point, the weekend and morning show anchors had been filling in for us for weeks, so the fact that "the anchors" weren't anchoring the news was news in itself. After several more weeks and with Sam on the mend, we went back on the air. I went back on first and anchored the newscasts by myself until he joined me a few weeks later when his family was in a better place. It felt like everyone was just waiting to see if we would fall apart. We didn't.

We worked together, covered our emotions, and took care of each other as best we could. Three shows a day, five days a week. That whole year is a bit of a blur now. Every night I could feel the strange energy in that one-foot space between us on the anchor desk. We both tried so hard to help each other, to cheer each other up, and to make it all OK. The viewers responded with overwhelming support. Our ratings grew. Sam continued to recover. We all survived.

I put on a good show, but each day was a challenge. At first, the emotional turmoil was overwhelming at times. I reported on tragedies and held my emotions in check. I would hear my coanchors phone ring in the newsroom and brace in case it was a concerned call from his wife. Each show was like a tic mark on a one-year sentence that I was serving. There were days when I would be getting ready in the mornings and stare in the mirror. I remember standing in my bathroom and holding my husband's razor and thinking, What if I just sliced my face up. Then I wouldn't be pretty. Then they wouldn't want me to do the news. It sounds disturbing now, but I wanted so badly to find a faster way out. The lesson for you as you go through THIS, is that I never took a short cut. You can't. I did the work until the days started to feel more normal and the mention of Sam's name stung less. During that year I won back the hearts of our viewers and they once again voted me Charleston's favorite news anchor. That local award by our city's paper meant more to me that year than a Nobel Prize. Then... one year to the day that I went back on air, I walked into the GM's office and told her I was leaving. I had set a target and I hit it. Now it was my choice. Looking back now, I believe that leaving on my terms was my only way to own THIS. It changed the narrative of my story and created a new strength in me that I couldn't explain.

Strange Superpowers

This sounds strange to write, but I sometimes feel I have a weird super power now that I have come out on the other side of each THIS in my life story and I know what they feel like. It is an odd courage that may make me take risks others will not. I would not wish THIS on anyone, but I'm guessing others who have gone through similar traumas will tell you that life feels very different when you finally come out on the other side.

In more recent years, I have found myself standing confidently in a room full of people in a stressful situation and taking the lead. As an executive in a high-growth software company, there are make or break meetings and presentations that have to go your way. I have watched grown men crumble under the weight of that stress while I just kept doing what needed to be done. When you work your way through THIS, you will have new strength that you cannot explain.

That is what you should take from this scary chapter. If you have those dark thoughts in your head, get help. You need to know that your future self will thank you. Getting help can be hard, but you are worth the work. When you do the work, and figure it out, you will discover a new version of you. You will have new strength that you never knew existed.

CHAPTER 9:

Writing a Script to Protect Yourself

When writing the story of your life,
don't let anyone else hold the pen
– Harley Davidson

T ime to share the most practical piece of advice I can give you. To get past THIS and to keep THIS from defining you, you have to actually, physically get out into the world, which can be challenging. You will have to get back to the business of living. To do that, you will have to be around people. Yes, other humans. You will have to go into the sea of humanity (in my head that phrase has a voice over of a deep ominous male announcer – THE SEA OF HUMANITY).

If you are dreading the thought of having to go back to work, class, the carpool line, or the grocery store where people will want to talk about THIS, and that thought makes you want to crawl back into bed, keep reading. I have a something that can help. Getting out of your safe place is a big step. This next tip may be the most important thing you take from this book. I learned it the hard way.

McAllister's Deli

A few weeks after the accident with Sam, when doctors were saying he was going to make it, and everyone was strangely ready to move on to a new story, I got brave enough to try to go out into my community. We set our sights on the McAllisters Deli, a few blocks away. With the prize of a big sweet tea and a BLT, I ventured out. The plan was that I would stand in line with my husband. He would order, and we would take it to go. That's it – just a quick outing into the world as a trial run. I remember that I wore a baseball cap and a big sweatshirt, sort of a shield from the real world. I remember standing in line. We were about five people from the counter. The line seemed to take forever. As I stood there, it felt like the whole place was staring at me. My heart began to race, and an overwhelming fear came over me. What if someone said 'How are You?' – I grabbed my husband's arm and pulled him with me as I ran out. I could not do this. I could not go out into the world. Maybe never! That is when I learned this survival skill. You need a script.

You Need a Script

One of the hardest things you may be struggling with is the people around you. Everywhere you go, people will want to talk about THIS. People will want to let you know that they feel bad for you. They are well-meaning, but it is so difficult because it puts the burden back on you. You will find yourself examining it all, and then actually trying to explain THIS to make them feel better about THIS. It is strange, but you will end up trying to make them feel better.

Here is how many of my conversations went:

"Hi, Nina, so good to see you out and about. I cannot even imagine. How are you getting through this?"

What I heard: "Cannot imagine, how horrible." My brain stuck on the word "horrible." My mind instantly replaying the scene with Sam, the tire, the horror, the chaos. Then I would ramble on unchecked in all different directions explaining, defending, falling apart each time.

With each person I encountered, I was reliving the scene, and experiencing all the emotions of it again. At first, I found myself saying too much to every person, explaining how horrible, defending everyone who was there, trying to make sense of it out loud with everyone I encountered when I couldn't make it make sense in my own head. Other times, I was irritated. I wanted to say, "Yes, it was horrible, and thank you so much for reminding me right now in this calm moment, so I can relive the scene one more time just to share it with you." I never said that, but I came close a few times. I soon realized that I had no acceptable answer for "How are you?" If I said "OK," then people would think I was in denial. If I said, "Good," they would think I didn't care. If I said, "Miserable," they would think I was just feeling sorry for myself and not Sam. So, I figured I was going to have to stay in my house where I was safe for the rest of my life.

The Sea of Humanity

If you swim in the ocean or you have surfed on a rough day, this analogy really works well, if not – I think you'll still get it.

One of the hardest things to do after THIS is to get back out in the world. You may feel frightened to face people, or embarrassed or ashamed if you screwed up. Or maybe you're just too sad and full of sludge to handle people right now. People do not mean to harm you all over again. However, stepping out of the safety of your own home can be like walking out into the ocean on a very rough day when the waves are huge. You are fine one moment, then someone asks, "how are you" or says, "I'm so sorry that happened" and you are hit by a wave of emotions because your brain relives THIS a little bit with each interaction. You will get to a point when THIS is not on your mind all the time, and you actually do need to be able to be happy in the world again. But after a traumatic plot twist, you can be standing in a calm spot, and then a well-meaning person can say, "How are you?", and the words pull you out like the tide and then slam down on you and swallowing you up like a crashing wave. You can end up being thrown around by the force of that wave, and struggle to come up for air. And then… as soon as you do find your way back to the surface, another wave comes. A simple "How ya doin'?" hits you and throws you back under. You cannot control the force of this ocean of people you will encounter any more than you can stop the waves from crashing on the shore at the beach. The people you meet. Just like those waves, certainly mean you no harm. They are just part of the ocean of humanity that lives outside your front door. Sooner or later you are going to have to step out of the safety of your home. People are going to ask, "How are you doing"; they are going to say, "I can't imagine" or that they are "so sorry" … it is what they do. You can survive this frightening ocean of well-wishers. You just need a sentence that turns the crashing wave into a large swell that doesn't push you under. You need a simple sentence that you have practiced so much it rolls off your tongue without having to think much about it. You need a script.

The Script

I actually suggest two versions of your script about THIS. One is for acquaintances, the people you really don't know well. The people you don't want to share a lot with anyway. The second script is for friends and family who are your support system. While you may not want to share much now, you need them to know you appreciate their support.

For me, the script I came up with after the accident with Sam so I could get back into the world, went something like this:

For an Acquaintance:

Yes, thank you for thinking of me. It is a very difficult time, but I have good help and we are all praying for Sam.

For a Friend:

Good to see you. I'm not ready to talk about it, but thank you for thinking of me and keep praying for Sam. It helps to talk about other things – how's your (family, dog, classes, job)

Your script should work for any situation. If you can start your sentence with "yes," that seems to work well. People want to hear they are right. To show you how this works, here are some scenarios in which a script is needed.

Embarrassing Event

Sometime THIS horrible event in our life is self-inflicted. Maybe you got drunk at the holiday office party, a girls' night out, or a conference in Vegas. These too need a script. Just own it and move on. Even when my daughter was a teenager and had an embarrassing event at a high school party, we came up with a script. She was sure they entire school would be talking about it on Monday. She didn't want to go to school Monday or maybe ever. She was sure her "life was over." We came up with a script that went something like this:

Girl at school:

OMG, I heard about Friday, how embarrassing. How are you?

Emma's Script:

Yes, I'm OK, it was stupid. I sure learned who my friends were.

Divorce

You need a script during divorce! Is it really necessary for you to tell everyone you meet the details of your marriage? These are the same details that you have kept to yourself all this time. During a divorce you may find yourself sharing intimate information and emotions with perfect strangers. You'll explain to anyone that you are in the middle of a divorce. If you are leaving or are being left, it does not matter. During divorce, many of us feel the need to explain ourselves and go on and on. Don't do it. Write yourself a script.

Friend or Acquaintance:

I heard you and Bob are breaking up. How are you doing?

You to Friend

Yes, it's a very difficult time, but we working through it. Thanks for asking. How are you?

You to Acquaintance:

Yes, it's a very difficult time, but we are trying to work through it. It is private, but I appreciate your support.

Lost the Big Game/Competition

I didn't have a script in high school after not making the Olympics. I wish I had. I didn't have many close friends at school, but I felt like everyone knew about it. They had talked about my world travels on the morning announcements for years. Here is the script I might have given my 1980s self.

Kid at school:

Well that must suck after working your whole life for it. You cool?

My sixteen-year-old self script:

Yeah, it totally sucks, but hey – I got to move here and come to this crappy high school with all of you. (Snarky smile) I'm OK. What are you up to?

Here's another high school example. The year our son Jackson went from JV to varsity basketball, he spent that entire summer and each morning before school practicing. The neighbors even complained about the 'bounce, bounce…clunk' noise from his 6:00 a.m. free-throw practice. He put in the hours and did everything he could to make the varsity team. When he didn't get a coveted spot, he was crushed. His friends all knew how much he wanted it, and he dreaded going to school. He felt like everyone would feel sorry for him. He needed a script.

The script we worked on with him, went something like this:

Jackson's script:

Yeah it really sucks, I don't want to talk about it, but the guys who made it deserve it. I'm gonna keep practicing.

A note on choosing to take a positive attitude: He made the team the following year.

Fired

This one is important! If you get fired, you need to stick to a script! You will be glad you did. I have counseled several friends through this one. Especially if you didn't know it was coming, things can spin out of control. Maybe new management lets you go, or there is a company re-org, or boss that just doesn't like you. Whatever the reason you were let go, you will likely feel rejected and hurt. You have to go home and tell your people. Your friends and family reach out to see if you are OK. Your coworkers may or may not reach out to let you know they are thinking of you. People will see you out and about on workdays and may say things like, "You're not at work – day off?" It may feel that there is no escaping this one.

The problem with getting let go is you likely haven't thought about this moment. You are unprepared to deal with it, and you have to think fast. All the things you say in the hours and days that follow will become your exit story. Warning: Some of the crap you want to say needs to stay in your head or be spoken only to a small audience, maybe a spouse, good friend, or family member who you can talk openly with and rant. Find that person and let it all out. To that person, you can say that it's unfair, that they have no idea how hard you worked, that Bob is not half as good as you and he is still there, that Joe is an idiot or that you hated working for Carol anyway. All of the complaints and ugliness that goes on in your head should NOT be said out loud as you are trying to make sense of it. Let it all out to someone you trust. For everyone else, stick to a script. THIS IS SO IMPORTANT. I suggest you come up with three to four bullet points and keep referring to those. Here's an example:

Bullet Points:

- Didn't know it was coming, and I am not thrilled
- Thankful for the time I had
- Going to move on
- Appreciate our friendship and any help finding a new gig

Example Scripts:

- I'm OK. It was a good ride and I learned a lot. The company wants something else, so no hard feelings.
- I wasn't expecting it, but I guess it's time. I'm looking for something new if you know anybody hiring.

- I'm not happy about it, but I'll be OK. I'll take my skills to the next place.
- I wasn't expecting it, but now I feel sort of relieved. I guess it was time to move on.
- Thanks for calling. Yeah – Wow. I'm still working through some intense emotions, but I'll be OK. It was a good few years. I'm sure there is something else out there for me. Thanks for calling. You OK? (This is a long version, but you can make it your own)

Try to manage your "got fired" script from the start. You need a couple of sentences to use for all those people who are going to call or run into you at some point. You want something where you are taking the high road, something that is still you. But it has to do damage control.

I am guessing that you will need to find another job, so remember that people will talk about what you say. Think about it. Someone in the office saying, "Did you call Bob? How is he?" then they repeat what you say. Get it? You can totally control this!! They will repeat the words you say, so write a script, and stick to the script. In this case: the same sentence over and over to each person you speak to is so important.

All the other people really want to do is to let you know they care enough to call and find out if you are OK. They feel awkward too. Just give them your sentences and move on.

Script:

Thanks for calling. I'm OK, gotta figure out what's next. I'll get there. How are you?

Here is some unsolicited legal advice for you – I am not a lawyer, so it's really just me sharing a tip here. If it's a work situation that has legal ramifications and it involves you talking about ANYONE other than yourself – be wary of the potential for a defamation lawsuit. Talk only about yourself – not about others.

Your Script Becomes Your Story

This script is so important because it does two important things for you:

1. You are the author of your life story. The words you use will become your story. You get to describe the event and your place in it. You get to choose words you are OK with other people repeating when they talk about THIS. You get to choose to share as much or as little as you want.

2. You control the conversation and your emotions. You will label THIS with words and emotions and those will stay with you and be repeated by others who talk about it. If you say you are getting stronger, they will repeat that. If you say you are never going to be happy again, they will repeat that, and it will repeat in your mind.

The best thing about the script is that it is yours. Come up with one you feel good about. Practice it. Let it roll off your tongue without thinking. My husband and I would practice mine out loud, making adjustments when needed. I would say it into a mirror before I left the house.

A good script can shut down a conversation. If you want to, you can use the script to end a conversation before it begins. You simply give them nowhere to go. I used this one a lot, and I am giving it to you now to use when you need it.

Other person: Any interaction about THIS

Your Script: I am not ready to talk about it. But thanks so much for asking. How are you?

For those who are a little slow or are just jerks and try to keep talking with you about THIS – Repeat: "I am not ready to talk about it. But thanks for asking. How are you?" This sentence can be repeated over and over and over. Sooner or later, they will stop.

Note:

Using a script does not mean that you don't talk about THIS. You need to talk out loud and let it out of your head. It just means you don't talk about it with everyone. Find someone to talk with openly. Someone you feel safe with, who you can talk with on your terms.

CHAPTER 10:

You Might as Well Make the Next Chapter a Good One

*"Hope is the thing with feathers
that perches in the soul."*
– Emily Dickenson

G oing out into the world is a big step and your script is a great tool to use to protect yourself in the Sea of Humanity, but you will need to talk with people again. It may seem like too much right now, but you will be able to do it. It gets easier to do when you are not in the thick of THIS. This chapter is about how you start moving your story into your next chapter. Like any good writer, you need a segue. I always think of the goofy stand up rolling machine that security guards use in the malls, but I am not talking about that type of segue.

A segue is a smooth transition. When you segue in conversation, you change the topic so smoothly that people might not even notice.

You can add a short phrase to your script to start your life in a new direction. To do this, you will need to think about what you like. This includes what you like about yourself, plus what you might want to change about yourself, and what you think you want to do next. When THIS is taking up so much space in your brain, it is hard to think about anything else, so here are a few ways to trick your brain to get started.

What Type of Dog?

Sometimes when a friend or one of my kid's friends from college is stuck in a moment and can't see past it, I hijack their defeat. It goes something like this...

College kid: "My life is a mess it will never be the same"

Me: It's going to be OK, this will come and go.

College kid: "No it's not, everything is ruined. My life sucks."

Me: What is your favorite type of dog?

College kid: (no words, looks at me like he would like to punch me in the face but doesn't even care enough to exert that energy)

Me: When you get older, what type of dog do you want to have?

College kid: Um … that's irrelevant. But a black lab I guess

Me: Well some day when you are walking down the beach with your black lab playing in the waves, you are going to think back to this day and be surprised at how much you let this tear you apart.

When you are in the middle of THIS and beating yourself up, it is hard to imagine an older you with something you like in a place that you like. Just that concept can change your brain and stop it from looping back to THIS.

This scenario can be done with any "favorites." Take food for example:

Friend: My life is over. I can't believe he left me.

Me: You are still your awesome self, you are going to be OK.

Friend: No I am not, I suck, life sucks, no one will ever love me.

Me: What's your absolute favorite food?

Friend: (no words, looks at me like she would like to punch me in the face but doesn't even care enough to exert that energy)

Me: I mean if you could go to any restaurant and have a great meal, what would you get?

Friend: I love that Italian restaurant downtown – they have a great wine list and the best saltimbocca, and I would have tiramisu for desert.

Me: Well someday, when you are sitting across from some new great guy ordering your saltimbocca, and drinking too much wine, you are going to look back at this time and wish you hadn't beaten yourself up so much.

With next chapter thinking, it is best to take some time and to start small. Think about some things you want to write into the next chapter. The idea is to create forward momentum. You are creating a mental exit door. To segue out of this current crappy chapter to some things that make you happy, you need some new ideas to work toward. It sounds simple, but depending on your THIS, it can be tough to see any happiness on the pages ahead.

I have a friend who lost her husband to heart disease a few years ago. He was her college sweetheart and the love of her life. Two Christmases went by and she was still struggling some days. One day when we were talking, she was holding back tears. It was just too much. She was exhausted. If it weren't for the kids, she didn't think she could even go on. Well, that was a red flag. How could this amazing, smart woman with a successful career, and two really great teenagers feel like life was just not worth it anymore? I shared that I had had some really dark times and I understood what she was talking about. As we chatted, I asked her, "Have you thought about what you are going to do when the kids are both off to college? Where do you want to be in five years?" She struggled to speak. She said she was just getting through each day and couldn't even think about that. Now reader, imagine that for a moment, she had been just getting through the days for more than two years. She was focused on her work and focused on her kids. She had not allowed herself to spend time thinking about a next chapter, it was too overwhelming to think about. She was staying in THIS very difficult chapter. It was wearing her down. Weeks later we would talk, and she said that that sentence changed her thinking. Where did she want to be in five years? She had no idea, but she decided it was time that she at least started thinking about it. A few months later she took some time away from work to figure that out.

There are a couple ways to go about this. Maybe you already have an idea of where you want to be in five years. With that five-year concept in hand you can take your new thought from Chapter 4 and add a sentence.

My new thought after the accident with Sam was: My life will never be the same. This accident has changed us all, but I am going to be OK.

I added the segue: And I am going to go back on the air (because I loved my career and needed my community).

Maybe you have no idea where you want to be in five years and are too caught up in the sludge to think that far out yet. That's OK. You can start small, with a simpler "and," and go from there.

This is all up to you. You get to decide the next chapter and the timing to start to move on. I am suggesting that since you are the author, you might as well add some things you like. I mean that only makes sense. At one point, when I was trying to course correct in my own life, I wrote down that I love being at the beach. I actually lived less than 5 miles from the beach, and rarely went there. I would sometimes go months without stepping foot on the sand. I decided that needed to change, so I added that to my simpler segue sentence: "and I am going to walk on the beach on Sundays because it always makes me happy."

What Makes You Happy?

To start to segue into your next chapter, you should spend a little time figuring out what you like. It may seem strange in the middle of THIS, but make some lists.

- Favorite foods
- Favorite things to do
- Favorite people
- Favorite places
- Favorite songs

It is sometimes good to list a few things you really don't like too, so you can edit those out of the next chapter.

- An activity that you really don't like doing
- A person you don't like to be around

- A place that makes you unhappy

I mean really. If you have an option, you might as well try to write a chapter without them. For example, I really don't like running. Can't stand it. I did a triathlon when I was forty-five. Afterward I thought about it and decided running hurt my body, swimming was boring to me, but I loved to cycle. So, I made up my mind to make that part of my next chapter. Now I have a garage full of expensive bicycles, and hit the road whenever I can. I join group rides. I do a few long-distance multiday rides. Some people act like other people get lucky and get to do the things they love. They aren't lucky. They just decided to do them.

Maybe you aren't ready for the big "and" yet. It does feel strange to be "happy" even for a moment in the middle of THIS, but I am giving you a license to find some levity. It is OK to have moments when you are happy, and it is healthy. Sam's mom and I got together in the year following the accident and told stories about how crazy we were acting. We laughed a lot. It helped. Right now in the middle of THIS, you can add something simple that will help you cope. It will literally send chemicals through your brain that will help you get through THIS.

With your list in hand, grab your "new thought" from Chapter 4 and your "and" phrase.

My new thought was:

*My life will never be the same, this accident has changed us all, but I am going to be OK. And – I am going to go back on the air (because I loved the career I was in and loved our community)

I could have also added little ands:

- and I am going to walk on the beach every Sunday
- and I am going to buy a new bike and ride one hundred miles
- and I am going to listen to Bob Marley songs more often
- and I am going to eat sushi once a week

Writing it may seem trivial, but thinking about these things make them start to become part of your story. These are the things you start saying to yourself and to others. These are the kinds of things you would want a friend who was going through a tough time to be able to do. Be kind to yourself and do them. Some of these things will start to come out when you talk to others. By simply using the words, you are starting that journey.

Another You

Here's one more way to think about your next chapter. If there was another version of you living on another timeline, like a doppelganger living on Earth 2, what might that version of you be like? It's still you, but different. For me, I like to think that on Earth 2, I joined Cirque du Soleil after college, and I am still flipping high above people's heads and performing. I have a crazy group of friends who also love to stay fit and go upside down and not take themselves too seriously. I travel and enjoy time with those friends. Still me, but not me. Some of those things could be me. Here on Earth 1, I did find some new fun friends who like to be active and a little crazy.

This is the thing with next chapters: You get to write them. When I finally left TV, I made some lists. I decided I did not want to be in front of people for awhile. I wanted to help others have success and be behind the scenes. I wanted to work a 9-to-5 job that would not call me in the middle of the night for a shooting or a house on fire. I wanted to learn something brand new and use my brain in new ways. That is how I ended up going from TV to tech. I chose those things to be part of my next chapter.

There are a ton of self-help books on reinventing yourself. You may want to read a few when you are ready. This chapter was a self-help cliff's note for you. During your crappy chapter, adding an "and" and starting to think about the next chapter can help you make a small hole that can grow into an escape door. You are creating a way to move away from THIS and toward something better. You are the author of your story. You get to add things, and you get to take them away. Write in the stuff you like! You can choose to write something amazing, and head in that direction.

CHAPTER 11:

You Are the Author

"All the adversity I've had in my life, all my troubles and obstacles, have strengthened me... You may not realize it when it happens, but a kick in the teeth may be the best thing in the world for you."
– Walt Disney

There are so many ways to look at THIS and to look at your life. I hope you are starting to see you have choices even during this crappy chapter. I will caution, even the best script, the best segue, and the most well-thought-out plans are just directional.

One thing THIS teaches us about life is that "life takes our plans and dashes them to pieces, sometimes once, sometimes lots of times." I read that sentence in Ego is the Enemy. It is so true.

THIS horrible thing that you are dealing with is uniquely yours. The ideas I'm sharing are to help you move past THIS, and start to write a next chapter where you are not defined by THIS. We all have heard of people who let hardships define them, like the parent who is still angry five years after a divorce, the person who still can't drive after a car accident ten years ago. Each person's THIS hits them in a way only they truly can understand. Sometimes THIS is actually a good thing, and some folks choose not to move past it, like the high school football player still talking about making the big catch in the big game when he is thirty.

You are going through THIS, and it has created a moment when you have choices. THIS is your plot twist, the point in the story when your main character is evolving. THIS is the conflict in the story that makes that main character grow. You are the author, and THIS has created an opportunity to change the settings and characters and to take the plot in a new direction.

It is an expensive price to pay if you stay in the crappy chapter. You could say it could cost you your life – the life you want. So you decide. You can sit in this sludge and let it rise until you suffocate, maybe stay in the house, and pray that things get better. Or you can start to take control. I wanted to give you a few tools and the coping skills to own THIS and to see past it. I know that it's hard and your story is unique, but I also know that THIS is an important chapter. During THIS you have an opportunity. THIS doesn't have to crush you. You can use THIS to become the next version of yourself.

There is a paragraph in Ego Is the Enemy that I want to include in full because it speaks to me:

"In fact, many significant life changes come from moments in which we are thoroughly demolished, in which everything we thought we knew about the world is rendered false. We might call these 'Fight Club' moments. Sometimes they are self-inflicted, sometimes inflicted on us, but whatever the cause, they can be catalysts for changes we were petrified to make."

Successful People with a THIS

If my story and the ideas I have shared are not enough, here are some other folks you may have heard of who went through their own THIS. They survived the crappy chapters of their lives and came out stronger on the other side.

Tiger Woods was the top-ranked golfer in the world for seven years and then had a crap-ton of personal problems and injuries that were on the cover of magazines all over the world. He took a self-imposed hiatus and then

124 | THIS IS NOT 'The End'

came back and won the Masters fifteen years after the last year he won it.

Vera Wang failed to make the 1968 US Olympic figure-skating team. Then she became an editor at Vogue, but was passed over for the editor-in-chief position. Today, Forbes places her thirty-fourth in the list of American's Richest Self-Made women.

Oprah Winfrey was born into poverty, molested, became pregnant at fourteen, and lost the baby. She was publicly fired from her first television job as an anchor in Baltimore for getting "too emotionally invested in her stories." She became North America's first black multibillionaire, and she is considered one of the most influential women in the world.

Steve Jobs dropped out of college (where he reportedly did LSD) then went on to become the cofounder and CEO of Apple. Jobs was forced out of his own company, started Pixar, then came back to Apple, and revived the company, which was on the verge of bankruptcy. (I'm pretty sure that was not his plan)

Steven Spielberg experienced anti-Semitic prejudice and bullying in high school. His parents divorced, and he went to live with his dad in LA. He was rejected by the University of Southern California School of Cinematic Arts multiple times. He started as an unpaid intern at Universal Studios. He's considered one of the most popular directors and producers in film history, and he's the highest-grossing film director in history.

Fred Astaire did one of his first screen tests and an executive reportedly wrote: "Can't act, slightly balding. Can dance a little." In the 1950s, he was let go from MGM when television became popular; then his wife became ill and died soon after. He reportedly wanted to quit, but he went on to dance on stage and in movies until 1981. He is regarded as the most influential dancer in the history of film.

Harrison Ford first took an acting class to get over his shyness. After one of his first small movie roles, an executive took him into his office and told him he'd never succeed in the movie business. Today, five of his movies are among the thirty top-grossing movies of all time.

Theodor Seuss Geisel, better known as Dr. Seuss, experienced anti-German prejudice from other kids when World War I broke out. He got caught drinking on campus in college (during Prohibition) and was barred from all extra-curricular activities. He went to Oxford for grad school to become an English teacher and dropped out. Later, he had his first book rejected by twenty-seven different publishers. Today, his works include many of the most popular children's books of all time.

Lady Gaga dropped out of NYU her sophomore year to focus on her singing career. She was raped at nineteen and underwent mental and physical therapy. She got dropped by her record label, Island Def Jam, after three months. Upon receiving the news, she "cried so hard she couldn't talk." Today, she is one of the best-selling music artists in history.

The Secret Strength

Almost always, the story of success is not the first draft of a story. It often comes after a crushing plot twist. The main characters in great stories suffer failures and traumas, and their struggles force them to build the strength they need to get to that level of success. So congratulations, you are going through a THIS. In a strange way, life just gave you an opportunity.

You get to choose which team you want to join. The team of folks who have let THIS define them or the rock star list of folks you just read. The ones who got through their THIS and went on to great success. Your call:

- You now have some tools to get yourself to a better place. I never said it was easy, but I did say I would help you get past this crappy chapter.
- You can change the narrative that is going on in your head.
- You can find someone to help and figure out the people and places that may be hurting you.
- You can put this in perspective. "Life is Long' and THIS is a percentage of what can be a wonderful long life.

- You now know that you can't go back. Unless you do know the Flash and have figured out the speed force. If so, call me!
- You know that it is normal to have really messed up, frightening, dark, thoughts, and you should get help with those.
- You know how to create a script, a floatation device so you don't drown in the sea of humanity
- I hope you now see that you are in control. That you get to write your next chapter

Through these crappy chapters we learn to respond to what life throws at us. If we do it well we become more powerful. That is the secret. THIS opportunity could be the most powerful change in your life.

> *"I don't regret what I've been through. I've had*
> *ups and downs, super highs and some really low*
> *lows. I've been so blessed that I could never say,*
> *'I wish this didn't happen."*
> – Jennifer Lopez

CHAPTER 12

Welcome to the Team

"One who gains strength by overcoming
obstacles, possesses the only strength
which can overcome adversity."
– Albert Schweitzer

Writing this book has forced me to revisit many tough memories. I've had to sit and spend time with them like old friends I am reluctant to visit.

As I write this, I am still working in a job in tech. I am a vice president at a high-growth software company. Most of the 1,200 people on the campus I walk around each day have no idea that these things are part of my story. They don't know I was a gymnast, don't know I did TV, don't know about Sam. I don't talk about television or why I left it. Sam is a healthy eighth grader, and I have watched him grow up and celebrated his life from afar. The love I have for him and his family is so unique. I still can't find the words to explain it. It is an odd love from a distance where I feel we are all safer. I can't imagine all the emotional health work they have put in. I feel fortunate to have had such loving, generous people go through THIS with me. That is not always the case. This is the first time I have shared my experiences of the accident with Sam and the painful time that followed. I could have kept it to myself forever. Most people who know me think I've had a charmed life and that I've been very lucky. Now they will know the rest of the story. I've decided that's OK. Sharing THIS is important.

I could not have written this when I was younger because I didn't have this perspective, and I may have worried that no one would hire me because, at times, I had a whole lot of crazy going on in my head. I can share it all now, because I don't plan to apply for another corporate job or hide the scars that make people uncomfortable. I am writing it because you are worth it.

I share it now because so many people are struggling with the public trauma that follows THIS. Social media has changed the game, and everyone is a public person. Over the years, I have shared my thoughts one-on-one and they have helped friends suffering through traumas. heartbreaks and tragedies. I believe there are many more people these strategies can help and I know I could never help them all one-on-one. I am hoping that sharing these thoughts has helped you.

THIS Changed My Parenting

Today, when my daughter calls from college in tears because the sorority she wanted didn't choose her or she's devastated that she bombed an exam and it is going to "ruin" her semester. I know that pain is real. Each call is a big event as a percentage of her life experienced (re: Chapter 6), These are big events for her and my heart breaks knowing she has to feel so crappy. But I also know that it is teaching her coping skills and that it is a fraction of one year in her life. It is a few pages of a chapter that is making her stronger. It is a crappy chapter in the amazing long-life story that I look forward to seeing unfold.

Parenting Jake Through His THIS

For teenagers and parents of teenagers, I am hoping this book helps your relationships. When my son Jake was sixteen, he was the pitcher on his high school baseball team and his elbow popped during a game. Being the child of two collegiate athletes, he had always dreamed of playing college ball. The doctors told him he needed Tommy John surgery to pitch again, and he knew that meant the college scouts would look elsewhere. Angry and sad while he iced his elbow on the back porch, he told me in a serious voice just above a whisper "my life is ruined." My heart broke for him because I actually knew the devastation of being a young athlete and having your sport taken away. He felt that all that hard work had been for nothing. All those sweaty long days in a dugout and hours in batting cages had led to THIS. I did the math, at sixteen, baseball was about 78 percent of his young life experience. It was how he identified himself. His friends knew he dreamed of playing pro ball someday. He had been working toward it since he was old enough to throw a ball. That day on the porch he could see in his mind all the college scouts in the stands that he had tried to impress, moving on to the other kids. His dream was becoming his nightmare.

I wanted to crawl into the big porch swing with him and hug him and say it was going to be OK, that he was going to be amazing at something else and have a long wonderful life, but I knew he couldn't hear that at that moment. I had to just let him sit in this sadness for a bit. Let him know I agreed, talk about how much THIS sucked.

I would later share my story and remind him an injury took my sport away from me too. We would compare our scars. I would say that even though it didn't feel like it now, someday he would be great at something else. That THIS was just one chapter. It was one thing he was great at, and there were so many things he could go on and be great at.

He was just sad for a long time. His senior year of high school was a lot of rehab and quiet times when I wondered what he was thinking. He tried playing ball in college but never regained the confidence he needed to succeed. I think the pop that he felt when he blew out his elbow haunted him when he was on the mound. Years later, after some Division 3 baseball and a junior college comeback, he decided baseball was over.

It didn't take long for him to choose something else he wanted to be great at. He got into body building and looked amazing. Then he became fascinated with the science of the body. That led him to want to be a surgeon, and today he is ace-ing his pre-med courses in college. He is in love with a smart, beautiful girl, and applying to med schools. I share this with you because he is so happy in this chapter of his life. I'm sure he rarely even thinks about that crappy chapter after his surgery. If I had told him that day on the porch that someday a new happy chapter would be part of his story and that his THIS was making him stronger, he would not have heard me. But I knew. I knew he had wonderful chapters ahead.

My Hope for You

That is my hope for you. I hope that as you read this, that something resonated with you, that it allows you to think of your life in new ways. I hope that the spark deep inside of you that you might think has gone out, pulls some energy from this book, and starts a new fire. There may be a piece of you that is so covered up by so much sadness and darkness that you can't feel it right now, but it is there. You are still in there. The dark sludge that is filling you now can be all encompassing during this crappy chapter of your life, but it doesn't stay. It exhausts itself, and you will start to surface again. When you do, you still have all the great parts of you that you did before THIS chapter in your life, plus the knowledge from THIS difficult chapter will be part of you. The new you won't be the same. We are a collection of our experiences, so you come out of THIS chapter changed. As odd as it sounds to use this term, I think that each new me came out with added superpowers. I'm stronger after surviving all of my THISes. I'm smarter about the people around me, and I look at my life in new ways. You will have those superpowers too. THIS is a really crappy way to get them, and I am so sorry we had to meet THIS way, but welcome to the team.

Acknowledgments

Some may think I should have kept all these thoughts to myself, but a voice in my head kept hounding me to share THIS idea.

I want to publicly thank my husband Ben for being the supporting character in my life story. He is the hero and the love interest in the book of my life. He got me through the dark times and to a point in life where it felt OK to put 'the crazy' down in writing. I am so thankful that I married a weatherman with a psych degree. Who knew I was going to need that! He continues to encourage me to be the author of my life story. If Ben's grandmother Gigi were still here – she would be so proud of how he loves me.

When I married Ben, I got additional supporting characters. A mother in law who was a therapist and father in law who knew business. They are two of the mentors in my life story..I am thankful for Ben and Jerri Pogue and their love and support.

My kids Jake, Jackson, and Emma are each the main characters in their own life stories. They inspire me and keep me thinking. I am thankful that they filled the house with laughter and silliness when I needed it through the years. They also were quiet and did their best to understand when Mom was having a tough day. I am so proud of the compassionate, intelligent, thoughtful adults they are becoming.

The toughest chapter of my life is connected to Dean and Caroline who endured and were changed by the same accident. We each found ways to best that nemesis in our life stories. Their kindness and compassion are beyond measure. Their life story continues to be one of community as they inspire others with the work that they do each day.

I can't imagine how my life story would have unfolded without the amazing doctors and nurses at MUSC who's knowledge, skills, endurance, and compassion saved Sam. I don't even know all their names, but I know words can't express the gratitude I feel for them.

Dr. Saylor will probably cringe at parts of this book. His cameo appearance in the long story that is my life is tied to so much character development. I am thankful for his focused kindness. His deep voice resonated with me like no other therapist's could. I am forever thankful that he didn't sugar coat the tough stuff and wouldn't let me hide from it. If he would have said 'find your happy place' I might not be here.

A special thank you to the Charleston community who embraced me from the day I arrived in the Lowcountry in 1992. Your love and support through the good times and the bad affected me in ways you will never know.

This book is a physical manifestation of the mental gymnastics that goes on in my head. It is an organized brain dump in an attempt to help others who are struggling. Which brings me to the deep appreciation I have for team who helped me write this. I am forever grateful that I was accepted to take part in The Author Incubator program.

The Author Incubator team is showing up courageously and authentically to help people all over the world.

Angela Lauria, CEO and Founder of The Author Incubator – thank you for sharing your knowledge, creating this process, and cultivating such a strong team.

My Managing Editor, Todd Hunter, my Developmental Editor Moriah Howell, and project manager Cheyenne Giesecke - thanks for making the process seamless and for being so good at what you do.

Thank you to David Hancock and the Morgan James Publishing team for helping me bring this book to print.

And my final thanks is to my Mom who brought me into this world after having three other kids. I'm so glad she kept the 'surprise'. I am grateful that she moved nearby to help with my kids as they grew up. I am so fortunate that we can say what we are thinking, and we are quick to forgive. Love you, Mom.

When I watched Alzheimer's take my dad's life while he still had so much left unsaid, I knew I had to write this book.

Thank You

Thank you for reading *THIS Is Not the End: Strategies for the Worst Chapters of Your Life*. If you've made it this far, I know one of two things about you:

One, you now understand that your life story will go on after THIS and this crappy chapter is changing you. Flip open the book of your life… what page are you on? You have the opportunity to be part of the unique club of people who fortunately or unfortunately become stronger through THIS experience. Don't let someone else fill all the blank pages ahead. It's your story.

Or Two, you are one of those people who jumps to the end to see if they even want to start reading a book. You don't have to read it all. Maybe just flip to chapter 6 and get some perspective.

I truly believe that when we share our toughest stories, others will be able to find something that resonates with them during their difficult times. Together we can create a more open conversation that can usher people through the crappy chapters of their lives. Do the work to make your story one that other people can learn from and then share it someday. When you do, don't leave THIS out.

About the Author

Nina Sossamon-Pogue has been a successful corporate executive, Emmy award winning news anchor, and a member of the US Gymnastics Team. She says that she is the result of the plot twists of her unique life story. As an author and speaker, she shares the highs and lows of life changing events to inspire audiences to envision their futures in new ways.

Nina was an elite gymnast representing the United States from 1982-1984. The first year Mary Lou Retton won the USA Championships, Nina won 'Miss Congeniality'. Failing to make the 1984 Olympic team, she became a top NCAA recruit and competed for Louisiana State University's gymnastics team for one season before suffering a career ending injury.

After graduating from LSU, she was hired as a general assignment reporter at WBRZ in Baton Rouge, Louisiana, and then in 1991, Louisiana Governor Edwin Edwards offered her a position on his press team, where she researched education issues and contributed content for the governor's speeches. She didn't stay long in politics.

Nina went back to television news and landed in Charleston, South Carolina as an investigative reporter and then evening news anchor. She lead the first local newscast co-anchored by two women, won a Green Eyeshade Award for environmental reporting and an Emmy Award for best news anchor in the Southeast. Her fifteen years in news took her from flying through the eye of Hurricane Andrew on a hurricane tracking plane to covering presidential visits and the World Trade Center bombing. She was voted Charleston's favorite news anchor for ten consecutive years.

During her time on television, Nina was in a devastating accident involving her co-anchor's baby boy in the family's driveway. Going from beloved news anchor to the person driving that car almost ended her life story, but the baby miraculously survived, and she and her co-anchor went back on the air together..

Following her news career, Nina joined a startup software company and helped grow the company for twelve years. She was the Vice President of Marketing and Communications during the companies highly success IPO.

Nina has held positions as the executive editor of a regional parenting magazine and was named a "Woman of Distinction" by the state of South Carolina.

She looks back on her life as a series of chapters and believes the worst events in our lives can create the biggest opportunities. She candidly shares the painful life events and destructive thoughts that accompanied them in the hope that the lessons she learned will help others see past the worst events in their lives.

Nina and her husband live in Charleston, South Carolina. She has three college-aged children who are her favorite humans. She loves her morning coffee in her kayak and walking the beach on Sullivan's Island to connect with the people she loves.

9 781642 798067